THE BUILDING OF AN AIRPORT:
PORT COLUMBUS

"AMERICA'S GREATEST AIR HARBOR"
1929

ROBERT F. KIRK

authorHOUSE®

AuthorHouse™
1663 Liberty Drive
Bloomington, IN 47403
www.authorhouse.com
Phone: 1 (800) 839-8640

© 2019 Robert F. Kirk. All rights reserved.

No part of this book may be reproduced, stored in a retrieval system, or transmitted by any means without the written permission of the author.

Published by AuthorHouse 04/10/2019

ISBN: 978-1-7283-0585-1 (sc)
ISBN: 978-1-7283-0583-7 (hc)
ISBN: 978-1-7283-0584-4 (e)

Library of Congress Control Number: 2019903579

Print information available on the last page.

Any people depicted in stock imagery provided by Getty Images are models, and such images are being used for illustrative purposes only.
Certain stock imagery © Getty Images.

This book is printed on acid-free paper.

Because of the dynamic nature of the Internet, any web addresses or links contained in this book may have changed since publication and may no longer be valid. The views expressed in this work are solely those of the author and do not necessarily reflect the views of the publisher, and the publisher hereby disclaims any responsibility for them.

CONTENTS

Dedication vii
Acknowledgements... ix
Author's Previous Books xi
Foreword xiii
Prologue xv

1. The Beginning.. 1
2. Aviation Interest Grows in Columbus: The Aero Club and Norton Field 11
3. The Movement Begins to Build a New Large Airport in Columbus.. 19
4. The Graf Zeppelin and Don Casto's Efforts for a New Airport ... 25
5. T.A.T. and Port Columbus 39
6. The Pressure Increased 47
7. The Location and Cost of Port Columbus are Revealed 57
8. Casto's "America's Greatest Air Harbor" 65
9. The Momentum Builds for Port Columbus 71
10. The Bond Issue Passes: The City Moves! 79
11. Ernest H. Stork Helps Design and Build Port Columbus........ 91
12. T.A.T. and Pennsylvania Railroad Are "All In" 101
13. Construction Begins... 117
14. Runway Construction Begins 133
15. Airport Lighting and Airway Signs.. 141
16. Progress in Airport Construction... 151
17. Accidents, Licensing of Pilots, Airport Rules 159
18. T.A.T.'s Early Formation 161

19. Port Columbus Inauguration: Opening an Airport 169
20. Women's Air Derby – August 1929: Port Columbus Promotes Women's Aviation 183
21. Selected Ohio Aviation "Giants" 193
22. Did You Know? 217
23. Endnotes 223
24. Selected Bibliography 239

DEDICATION

First, I want to thank God for all the help and strength He has given me throughout the writing of this book. I would be a fool to think that without His help I could have accomplished this work on my own. I am not a fool and I recognize that any success that is found in this book is because of His support to me. Dear God, "Thank you so much!"

I want to dedicate this book to my wife, Vicki, with love and infinite gratitude for her help in making this book a reality. Without her love, help, support and encouragement it would have failed to be. There were so many times that all the signs displayed STOP! Yet in a strong and gentle way she would help guide me around them to move on to the next step in the process. In short she just makes my life better, more fulfilling and stronger. Thank you so much for all you do.

I also want to thank Fran Savage for all the love and support she provided to me. She would read the manuscript and always have something nice to say along with important corrections and suggestions. She was always helpful. She is an author herself of four books and knows her craft. She also has a gift for making suggestions for corrections in the book that made me almost welcome them. She is a gifted and talented friend.

ACKNOWLEDGEMENTS

I have so many people to thank for their help in making this book a reality. It isn't hard to start but it certainly hard to finish.

First I have to begin with my "Wingman" in this project. Before I took on the assignment to research and write the book I told the backers in Columbus that I would need a wingman to help me with the hard, laborious, mostly dull background research that leads so often to rolls of microfiche that are next to impossible to copy and to read. If one is not in need of glasses before the process starts, one will surely be in need of them as the process unfolds.

One man volunteered immediately, Tom Kromer. Tom is a retired lawyer and CPA and I couldn't have had a better person on the job. I can't even remember the number of times I would call or email Tom and say, "Wingman Tom, I have another job for you." He never resisted but faithfully and fully worked with who ever he needed to work with to get the information for me. I can truly say that without his help and support this book could not have been completed in the year that was allotted to it. Thank you Tom for all you did, and continue to do, to bring the Port Columbus Project closer to a reality.

I had two other wingmen that were not named as such but they took on that role and helped support Tom and me in our work. They are George O'Donnel and Jim "Jet" Thompson. Both have tremendous strengths in working with people and in research. Both are very knowledgeable concerning Port Columbus' history and are connected with other community leaders that are also concerned and involved. Without George and Jim I also fear that this project would not have seen completion. Thank you both for your support, encouragement and marvelous skills.

I also want to thank others that played major parts in the real living history of Port Columbus and Columbus aviation. They lived the history in various fields including working in aviation at North American Aviation/Rockwell, flying for the Air Force and TWA and as a pilot and historian working for various state and Columbus historical groups. With this introduction I want to thank Nolan Leatherman, Don Peters and Russ Arledge. My greatest thanks and admiration go to all of you.

I also want to give my deepest thanks to the Columbus Metropolitan Library, Local History and Genealogy Specialists. They were always extremely helpful to me and went above and beyond to provide expert service to one living outside the state. I don't think I could have completed this book in the year allotted to it without their assistance. Thank you all so very much.

AUTHOR'S PREVIOUS BOOKS

1. *Warriors at 500 Knots, Intense Stories of Valiant Crews Flying the Legendary F-4 Phantom II in the Vietnam Air War,* AuthorHouse, 2011.
2. *Flying the Lindbergh Line: Then and Now,* AuthorHouse, 2013.
3. *Choices: Responsible Decisions for a Godly Life,* AuthorHouse, 2015.
4. *Warriors at 500 Knots: Duty and Pain,* AuthorHouse, 2017.

FOREWORD

I want to write a note concerning the restoration and preservation of the Port Columbus Administration-Passenger Terminal and the T.A.T. hangar.

My wife and I have flown the old T.A.T. Lindbergh Line several times in our small aircraft. We have seen what remains of this great historic aviation heritage and what has been lost. There are only a few of the priceless remnants of this once proud and contributory piece of U.S. aviation history. The T.A.T. structures in Indianapolis, St. Louis, Kansas City, Wichita, Waynoka and Clovis are all gone. And once they are gone they are gone forever.

T.A.T. structures do remain at Port Columbus, Albuquerque, Winslow, Kingman, and Glendale, California. All but one of these are in danger of being lost to history. Fortunately, the Disney Company purchased the western most terminus of T.A.T. at Glendale, California, the Grand Central Air Terminal and its surrounding property. Not only did they purchase the terminal and property but they spent millions of dollars on its proper historical restoration. They worked with the city of Glendale to develop the old terminal into offices for Disney but also a community center/open area that can be scheduled for community events. Disney set an example for all T.A.T. cities on what can and should be done to preserve vital historical aviation structures for present and future generations. It is my belief and trust that those working at Columbus to save and preserve the priceless old Port Columbus Administration-Passenger Terminal and the T.A.T. hangar will be successful.

Photo of Grand Central Air Terminal in Glendale, California. Restored by Disney Company and used for Disney Offices and City of Glendale community events. Photo by Author.

PROLOGUE
A Word About Ernest H. Stork

Ernest H. Stork played an amazing hand in the planning and the development of the new Port Columbus Airport. His contribution to this project can't be overstated.

One of his greatest contributions was the development of a pictorial and annotated record of the building of the airport from beginning to completion. The record became known as the Stork Scrapbook. Its full title is *Aviation – Columbus Builds and Airport: Port Columbus.* This wonderful, unique piece of aviation history was donated by Mr. Stork to the Columbus Metropolitan Library where it is preserved today. Much of the work of this book was borrowed, with permission, from this historical record. Reference for Mr. Stork's work can be found at the Columbus Metropolitan Library by using the book's call number: Ohio_629_1360977157_S886a_001. (_001 being the page identifier)

For clarity and convenience the author will only use the reference "Stork" with the last three numbers for page identification throughout the rest of the book. An example is Stork _282. This references the Stork Scrapbook with the identification number of _282. (In rare instances where the page isn't identified with a number, the author chose the next highest number and counted backwards.) The author hopes the reader and researcher find this helpful in their reading.

THE BEGINNING

The story of Port Columbus Airport begins in several isolated locations, at staggered times and even in different countries. It is the story of the development of aviation in a world not sure that it was ready for it and certainly not sure of its use.

The heavier than air portion of flight that became aviation's backbone began in a small bicycle shop in Dayton, Ohio. It was the Wright Brothers who began their work with gliders, and then with powered craft that resulted in heavier than air flight at Kitty Hawk in 1903.

Even though the Wright's first flight was only 120 feet long in distance and lasted just 12 seconds, it was the first long progression of steps that changed the world and set the founding of "Port Columbus."

The progression of steps continued in 1911 when Calbraith Perry Rodgers "successfully" flew his transcontinental journey across the United States. He was seeking a reward that was offered for the first travel of this journey in less than 30 days. Rodgers successfully completed his journey but did so in 49 days and only after he survived 16 crashes. He missed the reward, but set the stage for what would be the pattern for aviation's progress in the coming years. That was a series of large rewards established for courageous airmen who risked their lives to gain an award and move the needle of aviation progress forward.

One of the largest of these awards was the Orteig Prize of $25,000 offered for a non-stop flight across the Atlantic from Paris to New York City or from New York City to Paris. Raymond Orteig, who was a New York hotel owner, offered the prize.[1] This large sum of money was so attractive, like candlelight to a moth, that it captured the attention and imagination of aviators in the United States and Europe.

Those seeking the prize included the French WW I Ace Rene Fonck, with his crew; USN Commander Richard E. Byrd; Clarence Chamberlin and Charles Levine; WW I French Ace Charles Nungesser and navigator Major Francois Coli and of course a young American airmail pilot, Charles A. Lindbergh.[2]

The death toll of those who attempted to obtain the Orteig Prize began to rise. On September 21, 1926, Captain Rene Fonck's aircraft attempted takeoff at Roosevelt Field, New York for Paris. Fonck was WW I's "Allied Ace of Aces" with 75 confirmed combat kills. The nose gear of his aircraft collapsed on takeoff and the aircraft burst into flames killing two of his three crewmembers, Charles W. Clavier and Jacob Islamoff.[3]

On another attempt for the Orteig Prize, Captain Charles Nungesser and Major Francois Coli took off from Paris on May 8, 1927, heading for New York. Their aircraft, the "White Bird", was seen over Ireland but disappeared over the Atlantic and was never seen again. It is believed to have perished.[4]

Lieutenant Commander Noel Davis, USN and Lieutenant Stanton H. Wooster, USN were both killed when their aircraft, the "American Legion", crashed at Langley Field while on a trial flight for Paris. They were taking off on a practice flight for the first time with a full load of fuel.[5]

There were two major hazards involved in the non-stop trip across the Atlantic. One was being able to carry the needed fuel for the trip but also being able to carry the weight of that fuel. If more engines were added to help carry the fuel load then more fuel would be needed thus increasing the weight of the airplane. The addition of more engines gave an element of safety should an engine fail over the ocean, but the increase in needed fuel weight was a major problem.

The other major hazard was the North Atlantic weather. Rain and fog were constants along at least parts of the route and ice was also common during parts of the year. Aircraft of this era were really not capable to "fly blind" safely in the fog and certainly were not able to handle icing on the aircraft. All of these were deadly threats that took the lives of early transatlantic pilots.

"The death toll of transoceanic flights continued to climb. Since the fall of 1926… the toll had risen to 25 by September 1927."[6] Still other airmen continued to come to conquer the ocean flight and claim the Orteig prize.

The Building of an Airport: Port Columbus

Photo of American Legion Aircraft in which Wooster and Davis
were killed during practice for Transatlantic Flight.
Image in Public Domain; Image rights owned by the San Diego Air & Space
Museum which has released the image with no known copyright restrictions.

Clarence Chamberlin along with Bert Acosta were two such airmen. They had set an endurance record flight of 51 hours and 11 minutes. They had flown over 4,000 miles in a practice flight, about 500 miles further than needed for the New York to Paris flight. Thus, they and their aircraft were ready to begin the dangerous journey.[7]

However the owner of the Wright-Bellanca WB-2 aircraft, Charles Levine, replaced Acosta with Lloyd Bertaud. There were arguments about the change of crew as well as changes to the route and the equipment to be carried. Levine, then in a surprise move, took Bertaud off the flight crew. Bertaud obtained a restraining order on the flight thus slowing the progress toward the takeoff for Paris. This court injunction against Levine allowed time for Lindbergh to become ready for his trip.[8]

The weather forecast was also working for Lindbergh. Storm warnings had recently been issued for storms and fog over the North

Atlantic. It held up any chance of American airmen to attempt the start of the 3,600-mile non-stop flight. Chamberlin and Bertaud, as well as Commander Richard Byrd, had accepted the storm warnings and settled in for a few days delay.[9] Lindbergh continued to ready the "Spirit of St. Louis" for the trip and when a clearing of the weather began he was off. He took off from Roosevelt Field, Long Island at 7:52 a.m. EDT for the Atlantic flight.[10]

The story of Lindbergh's efforts making his successful flight is truly an incredible one.

In February of 1927, Lindbergh tried to purchase the Wright-Bellanca WB-2 from Charles Levine, President of Columbia Aircraft Corporation. Levine agreed to sell Lindbergh the plane but declared that Levine would provide the crew. This of course was unacceptable to Lindbergh.[11]

After a failed effort to purchase the Wright-Bellanca WB-2 Lindbergh decided to have an aircraft built for his exact needs. He contacted the Ryan Aircraft Company in San Diego, California and asked about building the needed craft. He was told that it could be accomplished and within the time constraints that he required. Assembling the "Spirit" in only 60 days,[12] Lindbergh went to California and worked with the engineers and designers at Ryan to build the aircraft that he wanted and needed, the "Spirit of St. Louis."

In comparison to today's aircraft, the "Spirit" was like a larger Cessna182. It had a wing that was ten feet longer than the 182, giving it a wingspan of 46 feet. This extra ten feet of wing provided additional lift to carry heavier loads. This allowed Lindbergh to carry the extra fuel he needed for the flight. He took 450 gallons of gasoline on his Paris flight. Gasoline weighs approximately 6 pounds per gallon, so he was carrying about 2700 pounds of fuel alone. This was an exceptional amount of weight for his engine size and it was this extreme fuel weight that caused so many accidents on takeoff and even in flight for those who attempted the Orteig Prize.

The Building of an Airport: Port Columbus

Photo of Charles Lindbergh (3rd from right) with "Spirit" designer Donald Hall (2nd from right) just after the aircraft was completed. Photo courtesy of Smithsonian National Air and Space Museum NASM 94-8819.

His engine was the Wright Whirlwind that developed approximately 200 horsepower (h.p.).[13] This wasn't a lot of power for his craft but the larger wing provided the lift needed to carry the weight. He could only cruise about 100 mph with the additional weight but it was enough to make the journey.

The actual performance of the "Spirit" was better than the designers had planned. The "Spirit" could take off in a little over 6 seconds and use only about 165 feet of runway to do so. It had an excellent climb rate and had a maximum aircraft speed of 129 mph.[14] Of course, this kind of performance was not possible on a fully fueled "Spirit" with all of the additional weight.

Lindbergh actually got the idea of entering the transatlantic non-stop flight while on an airmail flight[15]. It was on a lonely, dark, night flight, in marginal weather, that Lindbergh thought he could actually fly the ocean route if he could only get the aircraft that was capable of making the distance. He made his plans to get the financial backing needed and began the search for the plane.

Lindbergh was right, he had the training and the experience to make the dangerous transatlantic journey. He had flown as an airmail pilot in all kinds of weather. He had encountered night conditions, fog, rain, snow, sleet and ice all in his experience as an airmail pilot. He had faced difficult, even impossible odds, and remained alive. Because of bad weather, lack of fuel and other emergencies he had jumped out of four aircraft in attempts to save himself and the mail pouch.[16] All parachute jumps were successful with no major injuries to Lindbergh.

Fog was one weather condition that he would probably encounter over the Atlantic and it was a killer to many pilots. Yet, Lindbergh had developed the ability and skill to control his aircraft even in foggy situations. This proved to be a life saving skill for Lindbergh.[17]

The Building of an Airport: Port Columbus

Photo of Charles Lindbergh in front of "Spirit of St. Louis'
just before he took off for Paris in May, 1927.
Photo courtesy of Smithsonian National Air and Space Museum NPG.80.243.

Lindbergh was confident of the success of the transatlantic flight and carried very little emergency equipment. Yet, he decided to carry some for his possible needs.

"His emergency equipment list included:

2 Flashlights	1 Canteen - 1 qt.
1 Ball of string	1 Armburst cup
1 Ball of cord	1 Air raft, pump & repair kit
1 Hunting knife	5 cans, Army rations
4 Red flares sealed in rubber tubes	2 Air cushions
1 Match "safe" with matches	1 Hacksaw blade"[18]
1 Large needle	
1 Canteen – 4 qts.	

Lindbergh completed his epic transatlantic flight of approximately 3600 miles in 33 hours and 30 minutes with an average speed of 107.5 mph.[19]

He crossed over Ireland at noon and flew over the French coast at 8 p.m.[20] He arrived at Le Bourget Airdrome, France, May 21, 1927 at 11:22 p.m. completing the first solo New York to Paris flight.

There were large searchlights flashing over the field as Lindbergh arrived. A crowd of over 20,000 Parisians greeted him.[21] As the newspapers and radios announced to the world the accomplishment of the "Lone Eagle", as Lindbergh was so named, he became an international hero.

The President of France conferred the "Highest Possible Order Upon the Young American Flying Ace."[22] He became known as an "Ambassador" to the world.

Lindbergh was given a royal welcome in Brussels and given the Order of Leopold by King Albert.[23] President Calvin Coolidge offered to bring him and the "Spirit" back to the States on the American warship U.S.S. Memphis.[24]

After leaving Europe Lindbergh traveled to a breakfast in New York City where he received his $25,000 Orteig Prize.

Those with special interest in the development of aviation in the United States wanted Lindbergh's fame to be used for that purpose and avoid his being used to promote barnstorming. The Guggenheim Foundation arranged to sponsor a nationwide air tour for Lindbergh to stimulate interest in aviation. This schedule, along with funding, provided Lindbergh, flying the "Spirit of St Louis", to tour nationwide.

Lindbergh accepted the challenge and began an air journey of almost 25,000 miles. The Lone Eagle traveled to 82 American cities and to all 48 states of the Union.[25] This journey took over four months and ran approximately from late July to October 1927.

During this tour "Lindbergh completed 273 hours of flying time against the multiple hazards of ocean flying, souvenir collectors, unfavorable weather and fatigue due to almost daily banquets, parades, and pubic speeches. Colonel Lindbergh's program, arranged by the Daniel Guggenheim Fund for the Promotion of Aeronautics, called for a reception, two speeches and usually a parade and a dinner a day, for six days a week."[26]

He only missed one scheduled date during his whole trip when he became lost in fog and was forced to delay his appearance in Portland, ME. He began his tour on July 20, leaving from Mitchel Field. Within one week he had made an appearance to 500,000 people. Characteristically, he always flew alone to these appearances.

After Lindbergh's flight, other attempts at international flight continued. These included Lieutenants Lester Maitland and Albert Hegenberger's Pacific flights, Commander Richard E. Byrd and crew's flight to France and Clarence Chamberlin's flight to Germany.[27]

Lindbergh's accomplishments and his fame continued as President Coolidge decided to award Lindbergh with the Congressional Medal of Honor, the highest award given by Congress.[28] He was awarded the medal for his successful non-stop flight from New York to Paris.

AVIATION INTEREST GROWS IN COLUMBUS: THE AERO CLUB AND NORTON FIELD

All of these successful international flights, along with Lindbergh's visits to American cities and his increasingly vast popularity, escalated the public's interest in aviation.

Lindbergh included in his speeches to the American people the need for growth in greater number of airports close to centers of population, in order that America may maintain its supremacy in the air.[29] This, no doubt, had a positive impact on the public's interest in private and commercial aviation.

"Much of the increased interest in aviation is attributed by…the impetus given by Colonel Charles A. Lindbergh in his memorial flight from New York to Paris."[30] "Figures made available today at the Commerce Department, showed in unmistakable terms, the upward swerve of American Commercial Aviation during the months made notable by the record-breaking transatlantic and transpacific flights of American aviators."[31]

This impact was seen across the nation but it specifically was seen and felt in Columbus, Ohio. "… it is certain that Columbus gave but scant thought to its airport until the morning when the world awoke to learn that Lindbergh was in Paris."[32]

"Thousands see famous flier circle city. Electrifies huge crowd. No one can take that fleeting visit away from Columbus. No one can describe Columbus' feeling and no one could have done it except 'LINDY'. Circling around the A.I.U. building and darting south so low that everyone downtown could easily see them… swooped down and almost shook our hand at Broad and High Streets. Then… he and his plane again circled, flying south below the courthouse and back until he again curved around the A.I.U. and was off in the westerly breeze."[33] It was reported he flew as low as 300 feet above the ground downtown.

Photo of A.I.U. building that Lindbergh flew around during early visit to Port Columbus.

The A.I.U. building was well known to Lindbergh and other pilots who flew in the Columbus area. It had been designed to be visible at night at a distance to pilots in the area.

"The [A.I.U.] Citadel is America's first aerial lighthouse and the beacons serve a two-fold purpose. With a visibility of 80 or 90 miles from the sky, they are a guide for night flying aviators, who may shape their courses accordingly." *Dedication of A.I.U. Citadel, 21 September 1927.*

Photo Courtesy of Stork Collection: Stork _139

The interest in the development of aviation in Columbus continued to grow; it was seen in public meetings that discussed and laid out future plans for the growth of aviation in the city.

"At the conference at which aircraft men and laymen will meet, airports, pilot instruction, aircraft factory financing, and airway legislation

The Building of an Airport: Port Columbus

and control, and value of international flight, will be thoroughly discussed. The army and navy have already announced they will exhibit…"[34]

Plans were even being made to advance the expansion of night flying in the United States. The design and manufacture of the first airway beacon towers for night airmail flights was awarded to the International Derrick and Equipment Company by the government.[35]

Another sector had already been working for an airport in Columbus. This was a small group of men who had served in the Army Air Corps during WW I. After serving in Europe and returning home to the Columbus area these young aviators decided to band together, form a group and promote aviation in Columbus. One of these men was Captain Eddie Rickenbacker who was a flying Ace during the war. He was awarded numerous medals for his achievements flying in the war including the Congressional Medal of Honor. He along with about two-dozen other WW I veterans joined together to promote aviation. They formed the Aero Club of Columbus in 1919.

This group of men who had flown the warplanes of our Army and Navy returned to Columbus convinced that a great commercial future lay within aircraft development. Inspired by this belief, they had formed the Aero Club and sought to foster air activities in Columbus.[36] The membership started with some 25 former pilots and observers of the army and navy air forces. The "…object of these original chapter members was to perpetuate the memories and traditions of their common services and to foster and promote all future aeronautical activities in Columbus."[37]

Soon efforts were started to establish a suitable flying field in the Columbus area. They wanted a field where all kinds of flying activities could be held and promoted.

"…The members of the Aero Club of Columbus who had the vision and foresight to realize the makings, in 'Good old Columbus Town' of our place in the air industry. … to that small band of World War aviators, who met in the year of our Lord 1919…and put Columbus on the air transport map and who were finally responsible for 'America's Greatest Air Harbor'."[38]

This group of men worked hard to promote aviation and to establish an aviation center in Columbus. They wanted an airfield that trained pilots, promoted aviation and brought flying visitors into the area. They also wanted to bring the newly evolving airmail service to Columbus. Their work paid off when in 1923 they were able to lease a small section of land to be used as an airfield.

Many obstacles and setbacks were constantly encountered. Yet through perseverance and confidence, and with the financial aid of public spirited citizens, the Aero Club finally accomplished its major purpose, and on June 30, 1923 brought into existence Norton Field. The field was named after an Ohio military pilot, Lieutenant Fred W. Norton, who was killed in action in France in 1918.[39]

Lieutenant Norton was not actually killed in battle, but his aircraft was shot down and he was wounded. He was able to land his plane successfully in friendly territory. However, there was a two-day delay getting him proper medical care and he contracted pneumonia during those two days and died. He had been a highly successful athlete at The Ohio State University.

In 1926 the Aero Club built a clubhouse at Norton Field. It really didn't start out as a very good or attractive clubhouse. It was an old army barracks that was in some disrepair. It had been purchased at a government surplus auction for $1.00. It cost $350 to move the barracks to Norton Field. It became a common meeting place for transient pilots that made a stopover in the Columbus area.

Norton Field was a 100-acre plot and was leased for 10 years by the Pure Oil Company. "The property was provided to the War Department for $1.00 per year. The War Department built two steel hangars, a fueling dock and a beacon light tower. The first delivery of airmail to Columbus occurred on the day of its dedication.

Norton Field became the headquarters for the 308th Observation Squadron made up of local reservists, many of whom were members of the Aero Club."[40]

The Building of an Airport: Port Columbus

THE Aero Club stands for progress and community advancement in the fast approaching age of the air. Future civic benefits in aviation can be secured only by planning now to gain them. The Aero Club is the logical organization to look after Columbus' interests in this rapidly expanding field—and your support of the Club NOW will make the early achievement of its aims a certainty.

The picture above is a pen drawing made from an actual photograph of the Aero Club's beautiful Club House and Aviation Center at Norton Field. This *aeronautic headquarters* was formally opened with a mammoth two-day air carnival, August 21st and 22nd, 1926; it has the distinction of being the first structure of its kind in the United States and is dedicated to and maintained for the promotion of local and national aeronautic activities.

The interior, pictured below, is delightfully and comfortably fitted up and, in addition to providing accommodations for visiting pilots and transient airways passengers, is available for use by members for bridge parties, dances, dinner meetings and similar functions.

At the lower right, is an airplane view of the War Department's steel hangars, showing the "Norton Field" sign on the roofs, legible from an altitude of 5,000 feet. These buildings, together with the fuel storage house, field lighting installations and airplane equipment, cost the Government over $200,000.00.

Norton Field is a designated stop on the U. S. Air Corps Model Airway; visiting ships "drop in" almost every day from such widely scattered places as Washington, Dayton, St. Louis, Detroit and Louisville.

Pamphlet on Aero Club at Norton Field.
Photo courtesy of Stork Collection: Stork _014

15

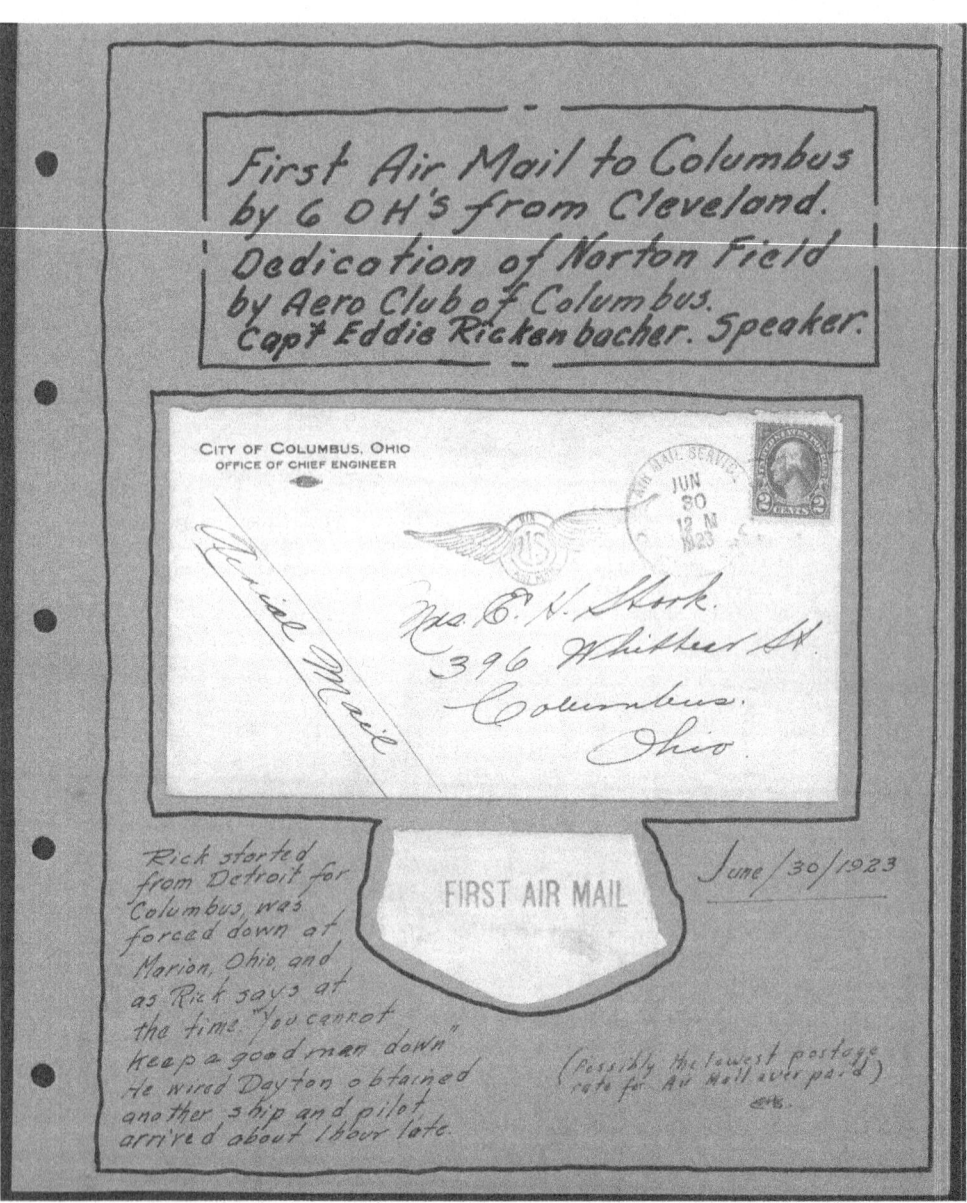

First airmail letter to Norton Field.
Photo courtesy of Stork Collection: Stork _008

Captain William F. Centner, wartime pilot, was formally selected as the secretary-treasurer of the Columbus Aero Club. He formerly held a position in the aeronautical division of the U.S. Department of Commerce and later became the Superintendent of Port Columbus.[41]

Many of aviation's early notables flew from Norton Field. They included: Charles Lindbergh, William "Billy" Mitchell, Jimmy Doolittle and Curtis Lemay, who trained there in 1931-1932.[42]

Norton served as a pilot training field during WW II with a civilian flight school. It served as a public airport after the war until the mid 1950s when it was sold for a residential development.

According to Ernest H. Stork the Aero Club at Norton Field did a lot to promote and help aviation in the Columbus area. He said in his airport scrapbook,

"What the Aero Club has done for Columbus:

1. Establish Norton Field in Columbus
2. Sponsored many educational flying events
3. U.S. Air Corps Reserve established active unit – "308th" Observation Squadron
4. Developed a Headquarters and Club House Building that helps-
    a. Social Center
    b. Passenger depot for transient air travelers
    c. Discouraging dangerous stunt flying
    d. Backed and passed legislation licensing aircraft and pilots
    e. Promoted Air Mail service to Columbus
    f. Promoted a new Airway, fully equipped for night flying, authorized between Louisville and Cleveland via Norton Field."[43]

Lifetime Memberships were offered to those who were interested in future continuance of the work of the Aero Club. Many of the aviators chose to take advantage of the offer that was limited to only 50 members. Two notable Lifetime members included Edgar T. Wolfe, publisher of the Ohio State Journal and owner of a Stinson Monoplane and James Don Shey, son of the Ohio governor.[44]

Other notable members of the Aero Club of Columbus included:

Eddie Rickenbacker
E. H. Stork – Designer and builder of the new Port Columbus Airport
Colonel William H. Duffy – Service Director, City of Columbus
Captain William F. Centner – First Superintendent of Port Columbus.[45]

There was another airport in the Columbus area. It was the Sullivant Avenue Airport, also called the Columbus Airport. It was on the southwest part of the city. It was a very small airport that had a cinder covering on the runways. It was used primarily for airmail delivery to the city of Columbus. It was fine for a small airport but it was too small to be considered for a large transport airport.

Norton Field was a little bigger, but it too wasn't big enough for a large transport airport. Also, there was no possibility of obtaining more land to enlarge the field. Two other factors made it clear that Norton couldn't be considered for a new large transport airport. First, the Army lease was going to be up in 1933 with little or no possibility of renewing the lease. Second, the Army had already let it be known its desire was to move from Norton to a larger, new airport that would be built in Columbus.

THE MOVEMENT BEGINS TO BUILD A NEW LARGE AIRPORT IN COLUMBUS

The desire to purchase land and build a large new airport in Columbus became a major movement. John M. Vorys, Chairman of the newly formed Columbus Air Board along with Lieutenant Frank McKee, Commander of Norton Field, had much to say in support of the idea.

McKee and Vorys said Columbus could make a name for itself with a larger field. They said, commercial aviation in Columbus was being held back for lack of a large airport.[46]

There were several "… speakers at a joint meeting of the Southside Civic Association and the Parsons Avenue Business Men's Association. The speakers were John M. Vorys, Chairman of the Columbus Air Board and Lieut. Frank McKee, Commander of Norton Field. The meeting was called for the purpose of increasing interest in the proposed $245,000 bond issue for acquiring, improving and equipping an airport for Columbus."[47]

Vorys stated that it would bring additional business to the city and that there were over 185 cities in the U.S. which were contemplating establishment of large new airports in addition to the 864 already in operation.[48]

Of course, these large numbers of "airports" in the United States were really landing fields with only dirt or grass strips for landing purposes. There were very few large airports that had hard surface concrete runways and taxiways with proper night lighting and weather services.

McKee went on to say, "Cleveland has spent $1,250,000 for a modern airport of 1000 acres."[49] However, it was handicapped because it was built 90 minutes from the business section of the city. McKee asserted that new airports should be able to provide hangar storage facilities and a lighted airport for night landings.

Vorys told the business leaders that, "The bond issue will be no burden on the city's purse. It will run for 25 years at roughly $9,000 per year, which would mean less than one-hundredth of a cent increase in taxes."[50] This was important information for the business community to hear but Vorys' next statement was most vital to the business leaders.

"Without an airport, the city in a few years will be left behind as completely as an inland village without a railroad, and even now, air business is avoiding Columbus and going to Cincinnati, Cleveland, Dayton and Akron," Vorys asserted.[51]

James L. Thomas, the Mayor of Columbus, was very much in favor of a large new airport in Columbus. He obtained approval from the City Council to establish a Columbus Air Board that would look into all of the options in building and funding a new airport for Columbus.

The members of the new Air Board included:

John M. Vorys – Chairman
James A. Maddox
Scott Wehe
Fred Atcherson
General Edward Orton, Jr.
Frederick A. Miller
Lieutenant Frank McKee
Arthur C. Johnson
Edgar T. Wolfe – Columbus newspaper
Harry Busey
B. G. Huntington
W. H. Duffy
D. A. Schryver
John J. Lentz
J. Walter Jefferey
C. C. Lattimer
George F. Shlessinger
Fred Tibbets
Kline L. Roberts
Stephen E. Ludwig
Harry Van Horn[52]

The new Columbus Air Board began meeting weekly with the Columbus Aero Club.[53] One of John Vorys' first talks to the Aero Club told of the importance of what they were doing. "There are two major considerations involved in the immediate situation…The first is the tremendous interest that has been awakened in aviation by recent developments and it is imperative that Columbus should not let a single opportunity go by default to take advantage of this situation."[54]

One event that always inspired the cause of aviation was the appearance of Charles Lindbergh. Whenever he came to Columbus or even to the state he would turn out crowds in the thousands. On June 22, 1927 the "Lone Eagle of the Atlantic" as he was called flew to Dayton, Ohio to land at Wilbur Wright Field and meet with Orville Wright, the Father of Aviation. They had dinner together later that evening.[55] After a short meeting with Orville, Lindbergh, as a guest of the field, met with hundreds of government fliers who greeted him and talked about aviation. He also talked with aviation engineers and discussed flying fields.[56]

Lindbergh was without a doubt the greatest stimulation to the development of aviation since the Wright Brothers' first flight. Just days after his meeting in Dayton, Lindbergh announced that a new major development was in the works for aviation in Ohio. He stated that a new proposed airmail and passenger service was being planned and that Columbus was on the route.[57]

"Columbus is included as one of the main stops on the proposed New York to St Louis airmail and passenger line planned by Colonel Charles A. Lindbergh, according to a tentative announcement made at Washington, Friday, by the transoceanic flier."[58]

This caused great excitement on the Columbus Air Board. It was just what they needed to build interest in a bond issue that would build a new large passenger airport in Columbus to keep pace with advancements in aviation.

This will be, "Essential if the city is to 'Get in on Ground Floor' of newest industry. I think Columbus should have a new airport at once," stated George F. Schlessinger.[59]

Some members of the board believed that the board should act slowly and take plenty of time in selecting a site for the new airport while others thought the new field should be purchased as quickly as possible.[60]

John Vorys, Chairman of the Airport Board, was advocating a slower approach. "It is my opinion that we must study airports of other cities, and secure all information possible regarding our own needs for an airport, before rushing into the purchase of a new field for Columbus."[61] He thought that since the lease for Norton Field didn't expire until 1933 that they had a lot of time to act.

Other community leaders thought differently, and believed the new airport should move ahead quickly because of the possibility of new opportunities.

Scott Wehe, President of the City Council stated, "The airplane will bring with it as many new opportunities as the railroad or the automobile brought in their turn."[62]

Guy B. Harris, President of the Chamber remarked that he believed that this was the age of aviation, and the people of Columbus should realize the tremendous possibilities aviation offers.[63]

William A. Stout, President of the Ford-Stout All-Metal Aircraft Company, expressed his belief in the current rapid development of commercial airplanes.[64] Stout knew what he was talking about, as he was the chief designer and builder of the Ford All-Metal Tri-Motor Airplane that was ultimately picked by Charles Lindbergh to be the aircraft of choice for the developing Transcontinental Air Transport Company.

Once again it was publicly stated that a new airport site needed to be selected and that Norton Field would not be a good choice. McKee stated that "…the Norton Field lease would expire in 1933 and that as a site for a municipal airport it was inadequate."[65]

The City Council decided to move forward on plans for a new airport as well as other projects for the city. They voted to submit a bond issue to the voters in the total amount of $3,125,000. "…The issues including provisions for a new market house, the airport, and a viaduct joining North Third and Summit Streets."[66]

The breakdown for the several projects that were in the 1927 Bond Issue included:

$425,000 for the airport
$1,200,000 for the Viaduct
$1,500,000 for the Market House Project[67]

This gave a total of $3,125,000 for the proposed bond issue. This turned out to be way too many projects and too much money without much groundwork.

One of the arguments advanced for the new airport was that there were already 40 airports that operated in Ohio, with plans for 19 more. These included cities such as Dayton, Akron, Cincinnati, Cleveland, Toledo and Canton.[68]

Another important component considered in the building of a new larger airport was the tremendous growth in the airmail business in 1927. As stated by Postmaster General Harry S. New, "…airmail planes carried 146,088 pounds of letters as compared with 96,925 pounds in April, the month before Lindbergh's flight to Paris. Every intervening month showed a gain."[69]

This was more evidence of how very important Lindbergh's flight across the Atlantic had been in the promotion of all phases of air commerce.

The proposed bond issue for over $3,000,000 was set before the people. It had some inborn defects that didn't bode well for its successful outcome. Even though the people of the city of Columbus were excited about the importance of aviation to their future it was not made very clear to the people the importance of all of the other projects that were added into the bond.

One other important issue was that the promotion of the bond was not as bold as it possibly could have been.

Whatever the reasons, the voters defeated the bond issue in November 1927 and those who wanted to see a new and vital airport built in Columbus had to begin again to advance their cause.[70]

THE GRAF ZEPPELIN AND DON CASTO'S EFFORTS FOR A NEW AIRPORT

Another huge advancement in the struggle of aviation to make its mark in history was that of the giant German Dirigibles. The large hydrogen filled, motorized airships were trying to establish their place in history as a vital section of aviation progress. The first of these giants of the air to attempt a transatlantic voyage was the Graf Zeppelin. The plan was for it to take off from Germany and fly across the Atlantic and dock at Lakehurst, New Jersey. It would be the "First regular transatlantic commercial passenger and airmail service in history."[71] It left from Friedrichshafen, Germany and flew west to land in Lakehurst, N. J. Dr. Hugo Eckener was the Commodore of the ship.

There was a crew of 40 with 20 additional passengers aboard. One of the passengers was a woman. Her name was Grace Marguerite Hay Drummond-Hay, a British journalist who was the first woman to fly the outbound leg from Germany to the United States. She was not a ticketed passenger and worked for the Hearst Newspapers.[72]

"The giant Graf Zeppelin will require from 45 to 80 hours to cross the Atlantic; exact route not yet determined."[73]

"On its route westward toward the U.S., the Zeppelin did detour south and was near Marseilles over the Mediterranean Sea."[74]

While the Graf Zeppelin made its way to the States much was going on in the advancement of a new bond issue for a new Columbus airport. One of the members of the newly revised Airport Board was Donald M. Casto, a Columbus real estate broker who was highly supportive of a new commercial airport in Columbus. Casto was a believer that publicity was an important part of any business and could be used with great effect to promote vital business interests. He was a master of promotional events to bring his real estate to life and was very successful because of his skill in this area. Being on the Airport Board and wanting to help promote the new bond issue that was going to be put before the people of Columbus again, he decided to pull whatever strings he needed to secure a flight on the Graf Zeppelin from the United States back to Germany. He wanted the publicity of his trip to spotlight the importance of aerial commercial flight in the United States and in Columbus particularly. He wanted to write back to Columbus about the adventures of a Graf Zeppelin journey and upon arrival in Europe visited airports and commercial air centers to bring back information on European Aviation Airports.

Passenger space on the Zeppelin was very limited and the chances of his securing a seat were slim. However, he exercised his vast political influence and secured letters of recommendation from many political leaders asking that he be placed on the Zeppelin on its return trip to Germany. These letters included recommendations from the Governor of Ohio, Mayor of the City of Columbus, and the Secretary of the Navy, requesting that he to be allowed to join the passenger list.[75]

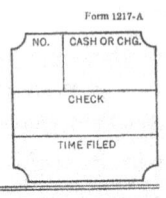

TELEGRAM   October 20, 1928

Dr. Karl Arnstein,
c/o Goodyear-Zeppelin Corp.
Akron, Ohio.

Don M Casto member of our Airport Commission has applied for passage on Graf Zeppelin to Germany Mr Casto has been extremely active in aviation activities and is a delegate from a large group officially representing the city Your good offices in having Mr Casto included among the passengers on the return flight will be greatly appreciated

James J Thomas
Mayor of Columbus

Charge
Don M Casto
36 N. Gay st

Letter from Mayor of Columbus requesting
Casto to be on board Graf Zeppelin.
Photo courtesy of Don M. Casto III Collection.

The Building of an Airport: Port Columbus

WESTERN UNION

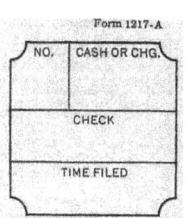

TELEGRAM   October 20 1928

Dr. Karl Arnstein,
Goodyear-Zeppelin Corp.
Akron, Ohio.

Don M Casto of Columbus prominent in aviation affairs has made application for passage on the Graf Zeppelins return flight to Germany Ohio is eager to have a representative among the passengers Anything you can do to insure Mr Castos place in the ship will be very much appreciated

                                        Vic Donahey
                                        Governor of Ohio

Charge
Don M Casto
36   Day

Letter from Governor of Ohio requesting Casto to be on board Graf Zeppelin. Photo courtesy of Don M. Casto III Collection.

> 200, 2 EXTRA
>
> HON CURTIS D WILBUR,
>
> SECY OF NAVY WASHINGTON DC.
>
> REFERRING TO MY TELEGRAM TO YOU REQUESTING YOUR COOPERATION IN SECURING FOR DON M CASTO A PLACE IN THE GRAF ZEPPELIN ON RETURN TRIP TO GERMANY PERMIT ME TO ADD THAT THE GOVERNOR OF OHIO AND THE MAYOR OF COLUMBUS HAVE URGENTLY REQUESTED RECOGNITION OF OHIO AND THE STRATEGIC AIRPORT PROJECT AT COLUMBUS BY GRANTING REQUEST FOR MR CASTO'S PASSAGE PARDON MY SUGGESTION ALSO THAT IN VIEW OF FACT THAT SELECTION OF THOSE WHO WILL BE ACCEPTED AS RETURN PASSENGERS IS LIKELY TO BE DECIDED TOMORROW PROMPT RECEOMMENDATION BY YOU TO DR HUGO ECKNER AND DR ARNSTEIN WOULD BE DOUBLY HELPFUL DOCTORS ARNSTEIN AND ECKNER ARE NOW GUESTS OF MR HARRY BISSERING KENILWORTH ILLINOIS AND WILL REMAIN THERE UNTIL NOON MONDAY IF YOU CAN COOPERATE IN ENDORSING THIS REQUEST BY WIRE TO DR ECKNER AND WILL BE SO KIND AS TO FORWARD COPIES OF YOUR WIRE TO HUGH ALLEN CARE GRAF ZEPPELIN HEADQUARTERS ROOSEVELT HOTEL NEWYORK DR ECKNER WILL BE THERE LATER I AM SURE YOUR SUGGESTION WILL BE EFFECTIVE ASSURE YOU OF MY SINCERE APPRECIATION OF ANY SERVICE IN THIS CONNECTION YOU CAN SEE YOUR WAY CLEAR TO RENDER WOULD ALSO APPRECIATE KNOWING OF ANY ACTION TAKEN.
>
> ERNEST H CHERRINGTON.
> WESTERVILLE OHIO
>
> THE QUICKEST, SUREST AND SAFEST WAY TO SEND MONEY IS BY TELEGRAPH OR CABLE

Letter from Secretary of the Navy requesting
Casto to be on board Graf Zeppelin.
Photo courtesy of Don M. Casto III Collection.

```
POSTAL TELEGRAPH - COMMERCIAL CABLES
            CLARENCE H. MACKAY, PRESIDENT

RECEIVED AT                                              This is a full-rate Telegram or Cable-
42-44 EAST LONG ST.    TELEGRAMS          CABLEGRAMS     gram unless otherwise indicated by
COLUMBUS, OHIO                                           signal in the check or in the address.
TELEPHONE: MAIN 3794   TO ALL             TO ALL         BLUE   DAY LETTER
                                                         NL     NIGHT LETTER
STANDARD TIME                                            NITE   NIGHT TELEGRAM
INDICATED ON THIS MESSAGE   AMERICA       THE WORLD      LCO    DEFERRED
                                                         CLT    CABLE LETTER
                                                         WLT    WEEK END LETTER
                                                                            16-30326


87 R19GU 18 2EX BLUE 117PM GET ANS

SA NEWYORK OCT 25 1928

DON M CASTO           473
       36 WEST GAY ST COLS OHIO

YOUR APPLICATION RETURN FLIGHT GRAF ZEPPELIN DEFINITELY ACCEPTED ADVISE
PROCEEDING TO NEWYORK QUICKLY AS POSSIBLE REGARDS
                     H W MAXSON
```

Letter to Casto confirming an invitation to board Graf Zeppelin as a passenger.
Photo courtesy of Don M. Casto III Collection.

Casto, as an official representative of the Columbus Airport Commission was granted permission to join the passengers on the Zeppelin back to Europe. A woman, Mrs. Clara Adams, was also granted permission to be a traveler on the Zeppelin and became the first American woman passenger to cross the Atlantic by dirigible.[76]

Columbus was placed on the Graf Zeppelin's tour and the city made ready to receive the visit of the Zeppelin.[77] However, the Graf Zeppelin was not able to go to Columbus on this trip because its port tail fin was damaged in a storm so it proceed straight to New York for repairs.

On October 29, 1928 the Zeppelin departed Lakehurst, N. J. for Europe. "Cruising at 1000 feet above the Atlantic at speeds exceeding 100 mph as she raced away from a southwest gale that threated to reach hurricane force."[78]

Robert F. Kirk

Photo of Graf Zeppelin departing the United States.
Photo courtesy of Don M. Casto III Collection.

The Building of an Airport: Port Columbus

"All's well," was a report sent from the giant airship. The Zeppelin spent most of the day "...dodging in and out of rain clouds, slipping around storm areas, and zigzagging to find more favorable winds."[79] She tried to fly a Great Circle route but found it difficult with the winds. She went to an altitude of a mile and a half high to try and escape the fog. But soon after she had reached Newfoundland she had escaped most of the bad weather.

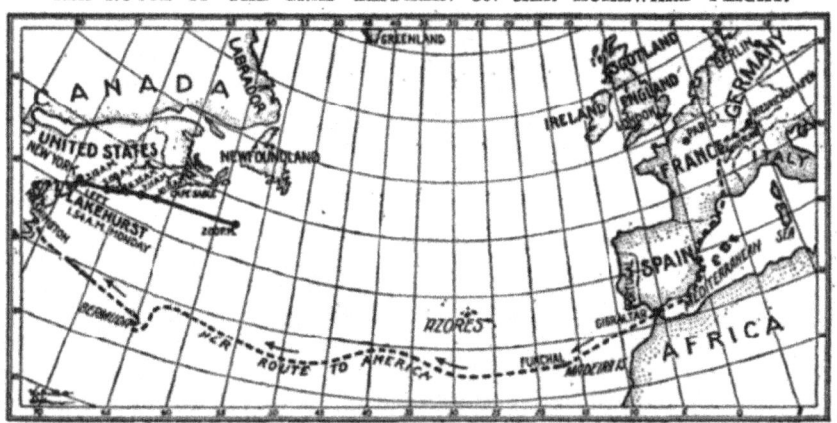

THE ROUTE OF THE GRAF ZEPPELIN ON HER HOMEWARD FLIGHT.

The giant dirigible's course from Germany to America and her progress on her journey home are shown on the above map. The last direct word from the ship was at 2:15 P. M. yesterday, but reports were received last night that several persons had seen a dirigible pass over Newfoundland at 5:30 P. M. If this craft were the Graf Zeppelin she had swerved sharply to the northward from the point where she reported at 2:15 P. M., in order to strike and follow the Great Circle route.

Drawing of Map of Graf Zeppelin beginning flight back to Germany.
Columbus Dispatch, October 30, 1928.
Photo courtesy of Columbus Dispatch.

The weather forecast predicted, "Good weather, with helpful winds, prevailing between Newfoundland and Ireland..."[80]

The "exact course of air liner is not known."[81] Because radio communications were very hard to establish and to maintain it was hard to know exactly where the Graf Zeppelin was. It had to relay information about its position to steamships that were in the area.

Casto remarked that travel on the Graf Zeppelin was "The most wonderful experience of my whole life. An experience that I would not have missed for anything."[82]

Yet, there were times on the trip that were frightening because of the weather that was encountered. He remarked, "At noon, we ran into fog, and plowed along through it for more than two hours. At 3:40 p.m., we were sitting in the cabin reading and playing cards, when suddenly the ship lurched upward. The nose of the Graf went up at an angle of 45 degrees. Chairs overturned in the cabin, dishes slid off the table and crashed to the floor and some of the passengers fell from their seats. A look of momentary fright passed over their faces, but shortly we headed back down. The ship was strong enough to withstand the attack of the elements however, and after a brief excitement things soon calmed down."[83]

Later the naval officers on board explained that they had hit a squall line similar to that believed to have caused the crash of the Shenandoah. The USS Shenandoah was the first Navy rigid airship. It was destroyed in 1925 flying through a squall line over Ohio.

Also off the coast of the U.S. the Graf ran into a strong gale. "We had a strong cross-wind and were battling a 100-mile-per-hour gale. It was impossible for us to make any headway in the teeth of the gale and the ship was turned directly opposite to its course and eventually drifted more than 400 miles from our previously-planned route."[84]

One very interesting fact about Casto's comments concerning the trip on the Graf Zeppelin was that there was no heat on the craft and at times it was very cold. Passengers had to wear their coats most of the time and Casto even slept in his coat one night. The entire airship was cold. Even the food was served cold. He remarked that the quality of food was good but that there wasn't very much of it. There were not magazines to read on board, only a few books. There was also no smoking allowed aboard the Graf. Casto thought that he and the other passengers would miss smoking but he and the others didn't seem to do so.[85]

Casto talked about how noisy it was inside the cabin because of the loud roar of the engines. It was hard for the passengers to talk with the additional noise. However, they adjusted by talking extremely loud to each other. After they arrived in Europe Casto remarked that his ears rang for two days after leaving the ship.[86]

Casto commented on the stability of the Graf Zeppelin. It didn't rock or roll and during the bad weather no one became ill or airsick. When bad weather did occur the Graf was headed directly into the wind and as a result the craft remained steady.

Casto was fascinated with the huge Graf Zeppelin and the experience of flying in it through good and bad weather. He was so moved by the experience that he wrote a long, one page poem about his experiences. It's named "Log of the Graf Zeppelin." A short selection from his work is presented here.

> "The fog is dense, we can't see at all,
> But on we fly, we hit a line squall,
> In a second we zoom to a dizzy height,
> The Zeppelin quivers, it's a test of its might;
> While in the gondola, we're all on the floor,
> Chairs, men and tables while upward we soar,
> We pass over the line squall none too soon,
> We have proven our ship in that moment of doom."[87]

One very interesting fact concerning the Graf Zeppelin was that not only was it the first round trip airmail and passenger service to cross the Atlantic, but it was also the first to carry a commercial commodity. A solitary bale of cotton was placed on the Zeppelin to be delivered in Germany. It was the first commercial product to traverse the Atlantic by air.[88]

Another interesting fact was that there was a stowaway on the return trip back to Germany. His name was Clarence Terhune. He was a 19-year-old golf caddy from St Louis. No one knew how he was able to sneak aboard without being seen and be able to begin the trip. Oddly enough, he became so popular because of his actions that he was offered several job opportunities once the flight was concluded.[89]

Photo of interior of the Graf Zeppelin.
Photo courtesy of Don M. Casto III Collection.

The Building of an Airport: Port Columbus

Photo of passengers on Graf Zeppelin including
Casto and stowaway passenger Terhune
Photo courtesy of Don M. Casto III Collection.

The round trip ordeal finally ended successfully. "Following a northern course, Graf Zeppelin, the largest aircraft in the world, today completed the longest eastward flight over the Atlantic. When the airship landed at Friedrichshafen she had been in the air, 71 hours and 12 minutes and had covered more than 4000 miles."[90]

"Great Trip," says Don Casto, of the Zeppelin ride.

"Arrived safely at Friedrichshafen…flew over bad squalls… in fog for 10 hours, hit 80 mile gale during evening. We were forced several hundred miles off our course over Newfoundland. On Tuesday we got a tail wind and it shoved us along at 80 miles an hour. On Wednesday we ran into three squalls 400 miles off the Irish Coast and were hit by headwinds which drove us to the Southern Coast of France. We passed over land at Nantes, France and flew above the clouds over the Vosges Mountains. It was a great trip"[91]

Robert F. Kirk

Photo of Graf Zeppelin in flight over the Atlantic Ocean.
Photo courtesy of Don M. Casto III Collection.

The Building of an Airport: Port Columbus

Photo of Don Casto during the Graf Zeppelin trip over the Atlantic Ocean.
Photo courtesy of Don M. Casto III Collection.

T.A.T. AND PORT COLUMBUS

With the bond issue defeat in November 1927, there was a renewed effort toward passing a revised bond issue and building a new airport in 1929. There were several factors that helped this effort move ahead. One was the rumor that Transcontinental Air Transport Company was seriously considering Columbus as the eastern most terminal for its newly forming transcontinental passenger service. A report was published in the Columbus Dispatch that the newly formed Air-Rail line was to make Columbus its "Port."[92]

Kline L. Roberts, Secretary of Columbus Air Board stated, "Columbus can't afford to neglect the opportunities now being offered in air development…Columbus must have an adequate airport in the immediate future and it must be municipally-owned."[93]

The rumors continued that plans were elaborate to establish a plane-train connection in the Columbus area. "Linked in the new organization are the Pennsylvania Railroad, the … Santa Fe Railroad, the National Air Transport and the Boeing and Western Air Transport companies."[94]

Like most rumors some of the information was accurate and some of it was not. One of the more accurate accounts was that, "The regular schedule from New York to Los Angeles will require 48 hours, with later service extended to San Francisco."[95] Also, that C. M. Keys, President of the Curtis Aeroplane and Motor Company and Colonel Charles A. Lindbergh were to be involved in the new company.[96]

Political leaders in Columbus went on record as supporting the new plane-train service company and were eager to see it a reality. Karl E. Burr, President of the Columbus Industrial Bureau stated that, "The Chamber of Commerce is making every effort to further that portion of the plan which includes Columbus as a point of transfer."[97] The Director of the

Bureau went on to remark, "It will be a great thing for Columbus. Our city will be identified with one of the leading and most modern industries of the Nation."[98]

James J. Thomas, Mayor of Columbus, went on record in favor of the possible plan. "The City of Columbus and its officials look forward with keen interest to the realization of these plans. Columbus cannot afford to neglect this opportunity, which will make it one of the most important transportation centers in the United States. This further emphasizes the necessity for an airport in Ohio's Capital."[99]

Photo of Mayor of Columbus, James J. Thomas.
Photo courtesy of Stork Collection: Stork _028

The Building of an Airport: Port Columbus

The Columbus Chamber of Commerce
Chamber of Commerce Building
Columbus, Ohio

May 1, 1928.

Harold M. Bixby, Esq.,
c/o The State National Bank,
St. Louis, Mo.

My dear Mr. Bixby:-

    Please accept my thanks for your letter of April 24th from which I note that as the result of your western trip the plans for the air and rail route, in so far as the western end is concerned, have had to be altered, although you still plan to make Columbus the eastern terminus. The latter is, of course, very satisfactory to us and we are hoping for a definite announcement from you in the near future. In the meanwhile no action has been taken in the way of raising funds or providing the municipal airport, our feeling being that very little could be accomplished before, while much can be accomplished after, the official announcement is made. I have, however, kept in touch with the members of the committee, all of whom are anxious to further the plan as soon as we are in position to announce definitely that Columbus has been chosen as the eastern terminus. I hope that that may be done soon because of the feeling here that the project has been definitely postponed.

    With kind regards and assuring you of our desire to go forward with the project as soon as circumstances will permit, I am

                                Faithfully yours,

Letter from President of Columbus Chamber to Harold Bixby, Banker, St. Louis, Mo. a man of great influence as one of the chief financial backers of T.A.T. Photo courtesy of Columbus Chamber of Commerce.

The realization that perhaps the rumors were based in fact and not just wishful thinking materialized when, "Representatives of the proposed corporation were in Columbus last week conferring with representatives of the Columbus Chamber of Commerce and the Columbus Industrial Bureau, as a result… Columbus has been tentatively chosen as the first port of transfer…"[100] This became the "Confirmation of a story regarding location in Columbus of the eastern air terminus of a proposed airplane-rail transportation passenger route," remarked Karl E. Burr, President of the Chamber.[101]

It was also reported that the flying would be done only in Ford Tri-Motored aircraft, those of the most modern type. Flying was to be scheduled only in the day in order to avoid the hazards of night flying.[102] This information was reinforced by the friendly relationship that formed between Charles Lindbergh and Henry Ford's growing interest in aviation.

Of note was the fact that Lindbergh had given Henry Ford his first ride in an aircraft at Ford Airport in Dearborn, Michigan. The aircraft was the "Spirit of St Louis." It was also the first time that the "Spirit" had a passenger except for Lindbergh himself. Lindbergh also that day gave Edsel Ford a ride in the "Spirit". When these two flights were completed Henry Ford readied a Ford Tri-Motor and the three of them, along with other dignitaries flew for about 40 minutes in the Tri-Motor. Henry Ford may have flown only one more time, that being on a Douglas DC-3 in July, 1936. This fact is not certain.[103]

The Building of an Airport: Port Columbus

Photo of Henry Ford and Charles Lindbergh at Ford Airport, Dearborn, Michigan, August 10, 1927. Lindbergh gives Ford his first airplane ride and in the Spirit of St. Louis. From the Collections of The Henry Ford; THF116264, Used by Permission.

Ford's growing interest in aviation passenger service was enhanced with this development of the Ford Tri-Motor airplane. It was built in the newly developed Ford Tri-Motor Assembly Plant in Dearborn, Michigan. It was there that Ford built 199 Ford Tri-Motor airplanes.

Photo Ford Tri-Motor Airplane Assembly Line, Dearborn, Michigan, 1927. From the Collections of The Henry Ford; THF115840, Used by Permission.

Ford also advanced an interest in the development of a small personal aircraft that was designed to be the aircraft equivalent of the Model T Ford. Ford was developing the idea that just as there could be a motorcar for everyone, there could also be an aircraft for everyone. The small aircraft that he developed was known as the Ford Flivver. It was a very small, single seat, single engine, low-wing aircraft. It was test flown by a young man named Harry Brooks. He was Ford's chief pilot. Brooks used the plane to commute back and forth to work. Henry Ford was very close to this young pilot and thought of him as another son. Unfortunately, Harry Brooks was killed flying the Ford Flivver off the coast of Florida, on February 25, 1928. The death of this young man, who was so close to Ford, caused him to lose interest in the personal aircraft concept and he stopped work on the project forever. "Harry Brooks and Charles Lindbergh were the only two men to ever fly this aircraft."[104]

Photo of Ford Flivver Airplane, Number 1, 1926.
From the Collections of The Henry Ford; THF9669, Used by Permission.

Ford Flivver Airplane

This is Flivver #1 (modified at least three different times from 1926 through 1927) and according to Otto Koppen, "the dimensions of the airplane were determined when Henry Ford told him that he wanted a plane that would fit inside his office."

The Fords' hoped that the Flivver would lead the way toward making personal aircraft more common. Harry Brooks, Ford's chief pilot, used the plane in commuting to and from work. Harry Brooks and Charles Lindbergh were the only men to ever fly this airplane.

Physical Description: Ford "Flivver" monoplane No. 1, powered with a 35 H.P., 3 cylinder French Anzani engine with a top speed of 100 m.p.h. Fuselage covered with black silk over wood and metal spars, marked in white each side: FORD. Tail marked: 268. Wings aluminum painted silk marked underneath: FORD 268. Single open cockpit has black leather covered bucket type seat built in. 356.5 square feet.

From the Collections of The Henry Ford

The growing belief in the confirmation that the airplane-train service was going to have its eastern most terminus in Columbus, if a new modern passenger airport was built, called for intense movement in that direction. Karl E. Burr, President of the Columbus Industrial Bureau stated, "The plan emphasizes the necessity for adequate municipal airport facilities in Columbus."[105] Burr went on to remark why Columbus would be such a good choice for a large airport. Columbus was uniquely situated far enough south and west to give it almost ideal flying weather. "Columbus is logically on the route on account of prevailing weather conditions. Investigations into weather reports for the past several years showed that this city had but a very small number of days when flying was utterly impossible. Fog and Sleet, the arch enemies of the pilot, are practically unknown here…"[106]

THE PRESSURE INCREASED

Floyd F. Green, Chairman of the City Airport Commission, believed that the announcement for selection of the City of Columbus by the Transcontinental Air Transport Company (T.A.T.) would be a reality very soon. "Announcement of a definite site for Columbus' new municipal airport will be made within ten days or two weeks."[107]

However, the final announcement of Port Columbus being selected as the eastern most terminal for T.A.T. became a kind of cat and mouse game. With the failure of the 1927 bond issue to build the airport there was a cloud over the selection of Columbus. Lindbergh and T.A.T. tried to make it clear that if a new bond issue was not passed to build a new airport in Columbus another city would be selected and Columbus would lose out.

Statements such as this one in the Columbus Dispatch tried to make the point. "Need of a new field was never more apparent than now, with the announcement of the selection of Columbus as the eastern air terminal of the New York, Los Angeles transcontinental rail-air route, and aviation enthusiasts of the city have been talking over the bond issue scheme with renewed vigor."[108] This statement was made in April 1928 but as of May, T.A.T. and Lindbergh had not made the final decision.

The passing of a new bond issue for funding and the building of a new modern airport at Columbus was a requirement if T.A.T. was going to pick Columbus as its eastern most terminal. This quote from Major Thomas Lanphier of T.A.T. made the point clear. "If the bond issue is not granted, our eastern terminal will be placed in some other city and will remain there permanently."[109]

There were other pressures mounting concerning the need for Columbus to build a modern airport. That was the growing interest in many larger cities to build their own airports. Already in 1928, "118 widely scattered cities in the United States have dedicated municipal landing fields since January 1."[110] That number was continuing to grow. "Marked increases in the number of commercial, army, navy, and intermediate fields during the last three months have raised the total number of airports from 1047 on January 2 to 1387 on October10. "[111] That was an increase of 340 new airports within a 10-month period. Adding to this pressure of larger cities building new commercial airports and competing for commercial business was the fact that eight hundred and ninety new airports were proposed, with many already under construction.

It was almost half way through the new year of 1928 and there was a great deal of angst going on within T.A.T., who had to have a new airport built in Columbus in order to place their eastern most terminal there. City leaders wanted to see an airport built for political and business interests and others promoted the goals of commercial and private aviation. All agreed that if Columbus was to be competitive with other American cities industrially and business wise, then a new modern airport would very quickly have to be approved and constructed.

The Columbus Sunday Dispatch, June 24, 1928 stated in a headline,"Civic Clubs Promise Assistance in Air Port Plans." The article went on to say, "Aviation: Appointment of New Air Board is Aim at City Progress…The group is composed of aggressive business and professional men who will do everything in their power to foster the airport movement."[112]

The Columbus City Council took steps to increase the number of those on the Airport Committee. "Legislation to increase the Airport Committee of Columbus from five to fifteen members will be placed before the city council as another step toward an intensive campaign for a municipal airport. The committee is now composed of three councilmen, Floyd Green, chairman, Henry Worley and Frank Karns, and City Service Director, W. H. Duffy, and Kline Roberts, secretary of the Columbus Board."[113] Henry Worley went on to become mayor of Columbus.

The search for the location of the new Columbus Airport was also underway. "Things are really moving toward an airport in Columbus. Within the past week, three famous fliers have been in the city and each of them voiced the plea for adequate landing facilities. One of them, Colonel Charles A. Lindbergh…declared that Norton Field was too small."[114] The other two famous pilots that were listed in the article were, like Lindbergh,

The Building of an Airport: Port Columbus

connected with T.A.T. and had a great interest in seeing Columbus build a new modern airport.

James T. Daniels, General Secretary of the Columbus Chamber of Commerce made two major announcements. They were:

"An intensive campaign is being planned to bring before the voters of the city the necessity of providing a municipal airport." He also announced, "…that Columbus has been made one of the main links in the newly-organized coast-to-coast railway and airplane system, emphasizes more than ever the need of a municipally-owned aviation field."[115]

A new Air Board was named and became a Committee of 15 who studied the airport needs for Columbus.

The names of the Committee of 15 were:

1. Councilman Floyd F. Green – Chairman
2. Kline L. Roberts – Secretary
3. Councilman Henry W. Worley
4. Councilman Frank C. Karns
5. Edgar T. Wolfe – Ohio State Journal
6. Attorney John M. Vorys
7. Alexander F. Hammond – H.C. Glorman Co.
8. Robert Lazarus – F & R Lazarus Co.
9. Malcolm D. Jeffrey – Jeffrey Manufacturing Co.
10. B. G. Huntington – Huntington National Bank
11. John A. Kelly – Citizens Trust & Savings Bank
12. Don M. Casto – Realtor
13. Stanley M. Ross – Moores and Ross Milk Co.
14. Emil E. Watson – Actuary
15. Clare E. Cook – Columbus Industrial Bureau[116]

Their duties were to decide if "Columbus should determine whether or not we are to have a landing field, inasmuch as Norton Field is privately owned and much too small to meet the demands of aerial transportation."[117]

While the push for a new airport in Columbus continued, Charles Lindbergh, the most famous aviator in the world, continued to make news. He placed the "Spirit of St. Louis" into the Smithsonian Museum. It was accomplished in May the same month that he had flown the Atlantic a year earlier. He had just short of 500 flying hours in the "Spirit" which was a lot of flying time to log in one year. The "Spirit" was replaced by the Ryan Airplane Company with a Ryan Brougham that was very similar to the "Spirit" except it had less fuel capacity but had room for three passengers and the pilot. Lindbergh's position with T.A.T. and his legendary status in aviation made him a very influential voice on decisions that were made with the Columbus leaders.[118]

The Airport Commission reported that, "Action, rather than publicity, has been the slogan of the Columbus Airport Commission since its appointment, ..." stated Chairman Floyd Green. [119] "The group gathered all possible data on a number of fields and decided on one... Members of the airport commission have investigated all angles in particular the three major phases which must be considered in our present plans, the:

1. cities welfare
2. requirements of air transport passengers and operators
3. possible industrial advantages to be gained

...Consideration must be given those transport lines that are assured for the immediate future, such as the important T.A.T. organization by the most powerful interest in the field of aviation. Definite arrangements have been made with this organization to use Columbus as its eastern air terminal..."[120]

Green went on to tell of the influence of T.A.T.'s leadership. "The company is headed by C.M. Keys, president of the Curtis Motor and Airplane Industries. Keys is also chairman of the board and principal stockholder of the National Air Transport Company, which is the largest operator of mail lines, with four years experience in flying the transcontinental mail from New York to Cleveland to Chicago and thence west."[121]

Because of T.A.T.'s vast experience in aviation the Airport Commission relied on their expertise regarding several areas of the new airport. One of the consulting engineers of T.A.T. predicted that Columbus must be prepared to take care of 500 planes on its municipal airport within two years. Therefore the new airport would need at least 600 acres because an airport of less than 600 acres would not be adequate.[122]

T.A.T. aviation experts continued to give needed advice to the committee. "Experience in airport construction has established drainage as the most important factor in obtaining satisfactory results. The question of drainage and landing surfaces, therefore, has been almost a determining factor in considering sites for the Columbus airport."[123]

Two other factors were important and considered as the committee looked for the ideal airport site. One of these was meteorological conditions. To be ideal the airport should be out of any prevalent ice or sleet areas. These areas are very dangerous for aircraft to fly through. These conditions also increase the down time for aircraft grounded during the bad weather. Columbus was south of these areas thus making it an ideal place to establish a major airport.

The other factor to be considered was the location of the field relative to the city. The field must be close enough for easy access, far enough away to make cost of the field reasonable, and make noise reduction and safety to the public a factor. The location that was getting most of the attention, and became the location for Port Columbus, was within six miles of Broad and High Streets.

Another recommendation made by the T.A.T. consultants was that the field runways should be at least 100 feet wide. Even a 75-foot runway width was not considered wide enough.

The recommendations from the Airport Committee were submitted to "…Colonel Charles A. Lindbergh, Chairman of the Technical Committee of T.A.T.… he approved the plans in their entirety, and revealed the amount of work that has to be accomplished,"[124] before Port Columbus was ready to open.

Photo of Columbus community leaders welcoming
Charles Lindbergh to Columbus.
Leaders (left to right) include Columbus Mayor George J. Karb, Don
L. Tobin, Edgar T. Wolfe and Charles Lindbergh. Lindbergh (T.A.T.
representative) was visiting Columbus to discuss the building of a new airport.
Columbus Evening Dispatch, October, 1928.
Photo courtesy of Columbus Dispatch.

The Building of an Airport: Port Columbus

Photo of Edgar T. Wolfe Sr.'s (1893 – 1957) personal aircraft. Wolfe was a Columbus civic leader and aviation enthusiast. His aircraft was a Stinson J-5. He would loan it to the Port Columbus airport commission whenever needed. Notice the lettering on the side of the aircraft which reads, "Port Columbus, America's Greatest Air Harbor." He served on the airport commission and provided it leadership and vision.
Columbus Dispatch, 1929
Photo courtesy of Columbus Dispatch.

Before the airport could even be started a bond issue election had to be placed before the people and passed. The elected officials had learned a lot by the failed bond issue that was voted on in November 1927. Those involved in putting together that bond placed too many items on the ballot with the new airport. This pushed the cost of the bond issue too high to be justified to the voters. It also diminished the importance of the building of a new airport. This time around it was decided that only the airport would be placed on the ballot and the cost of the bond reduced to just what was needed for its construction.

The community leaders also recognized that they needed to get more people involved in leadership to promote the new airport. It was decided that a large group of community members with various levels of influence should be placed on the committee to purchase land and build an airport.

Former Mayor George J. Karb was placed as the head of the group and was given the responsibility to set its number of members and its organization. "…Karb [was] placed at the head of citizens' Group with scores of sub-committees to acquaint the city with necessity of movement. More than 300 Columbus men and women, representing every section of the city…have formed themselves into a metropolitan committee to urge approval of the $850,000 airport bond issue November 6… Leaders of the movement declare the entire industrial future of the city may hinge upon passage of the present bond issue…"[125]

Don M. Casto was one of the members of this Citizens' Group.

The Leaders of the airport movement released information that "The airport bond issue will be again put up to the voters, next November. City Officials, realizing the importance of the issue, have intimated that no other large bond issues will be on the ballot…"[126]

The hopes were high for the passing of the bond issue this time around.

"If public sentiment and the opinion of the man on the street are guides worth following, Columbus will have a municipally owned airport within another year," stated Frank A. Petrie.[127] He went on to say, "An airport is now a necessity in any city, and doubly so in our own case. Colonel Charles A. Lindbergh is to be connected with the route, and will undoubtedly be here himself…to urge voters to provide adequate facilities for the air commerce of the future."[128]

More and more of the leaders and the public began to realize how important a new airport was to the future of commerce in Columbus. New industry would come to the area if an airport were built.

One such industry leader, Henry B. Watkins, General Manager of the Kilgore Manufacturing Co. of Westerville which operated several industrial plants," advised officials of the Columbus airport bond issue committee that if voters authorize the proposed municipal airport…they will probably concentrate in the Columbus area the manufacture of their new line of airplane flares for night landing."[129] He went on to say, "If Columbus voters authorize the bond issue…it will mean rapid development of the city as one of the country's greatest aviation centers."[130]

George J. Karb, Chairman, Citizens' Committee said, "We are receiving assurances everyday that if Columbus…captures its air traffic advantages, the growing aviation manufacturing will come to Columbus."[131]

THE LOCATION AND COST OF PORT COLUMBUS ARE REVEALED

As time moved closer to the November bond issue vote, more information about the airport's location and cost began to be revealed. Where was the new airport going to be?

"On the high, level plateau adjacent to the Army Reserve Depot, bounded on the north and west by James Pike, on the east by Poth Road and on the south by the B & O and Pennsylvania tracks – 15 minutes from Broad and High."[132]

A map was published in the newspaper showing the location of the proposed new airport.

Concerning the cost of the airport and the bond issue, the "Council favors $850,000 airport; Bond Issue will be placed on ballot providing $330,000 for purchase of land and $250,000 for equipment. Want 1,000 acres."[133]

Lindbergh remarked on the growth of business through the airport. "And where one plane leaves its terminal now, business will increase to such an extent that whole fleets will leave on schedule."[134]

"With the way paved for Columbus to secure an airport that will place it at the top of the list as an Inland Air Center with passage by the city council… an ordinance authorizing placing of an $850,000 bond issue on the ballot at the November election, the matter is up to the voters… but the help of the Aero Club, service clubs and aviation fans will be needed to procure the necessary votes."[135] It was realized that if the new bond issue was to pass the vote by its citizens then a lot of work had to be done by those interested in seeing the airport built. Yet it was believed that the passing of the bond issue and building of the airport was a vital concern to promote not just aviation but manufacturing and industry. "Feeder and taxi lines will spring up and that Columbus will be chosen as a manufacturing site by one or more of the countries largest aircraft manufacturers…"[136]

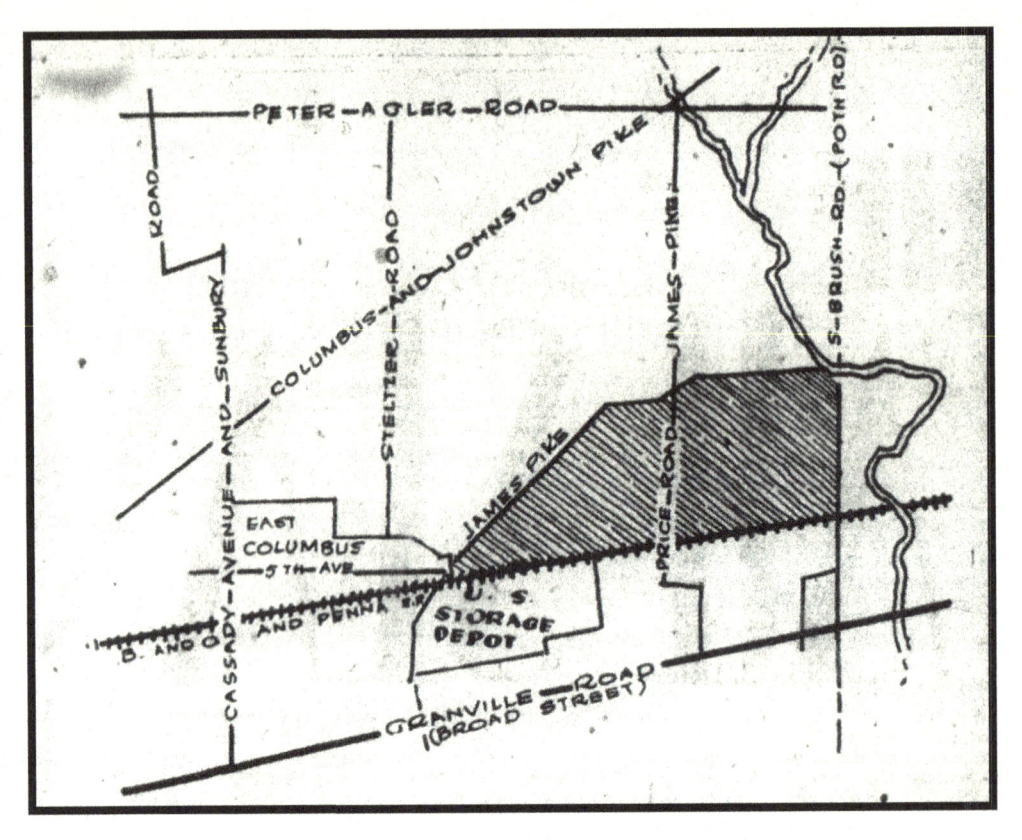

Drawing of the location site of proposed new airport in Columbus.
Columbus Evening Dispatch, September 10, 1928.
Photo courtesy of Columbus Dispatch.

Yet, this note to promote progress came with a warning from Charles "Casey" Jones, Vice President of Curtis Company and representative of T.A.T. "…and if this city is not in a position to adequately receive T.A.T., another city in this vicinity will be chosen as the eastern air terminus."[137]

Several newspaper cartoons were placed in the paper trying to show that the struggle for the new airport was a struggle of the past with the future.

The Building of an Airport: Port Columbus

Cartoon of City Council feeding airport plans to public.
Columbus Dispatch, September 7, 1928.
Photo courtesy of Columbus Dispatch.

Robert F. Kirk

Cartoon of Train Travel vs Plane Travel: 1928 vs 1929.
Columbus Dispatch, January 1, 1929.
Photo courtesy of Columbus Dispatch.

The progress of aviation and its place in the minds of citizens of the country were changing. Once it was the view that flying was reckless, dangerous and could only be enjoyed by those with an adventurous spirit. That view was changing with successes like Lindbergh's transatlantic trip

The Building of an Airport: Port Columbus

and his aviation tour around the United States. Statements such as this were common, "Flying, in short has ceased to being a novelty throughout the entire world, and is rapidly coming to be accepted as a customary mode of travel in almost every civilized country."[138]

To build on this change of perception T.A.T. and Ford decided to bring their huge Tri-Motor aircraft to Columbus and give free rides to the public to get them excited about passing the bond issue.

A Ford Tri-Motor landed at Norton Field, and during a ceremony, was christened "Columbus". This aircraft went on to fill several roles in T.A.T. service.

"A Ford Tri-Motor all-metal monoplane of the type purchased by Transcontinental Air Transport for use on its New York – Los Angeles railplane passenger service will arrive at Norton Field…carrying prominent citizens and officials over the city and the proposed airport site. The plane… will carry passengers on a 25-mile route around Columbus. Invitations to representative citizens to ride in the ship have been issued by Kline L. Roberts, secretary of the airport commission…during the visit hundreds of Columbus people are expected to cruise over the city in the big plane."[139] In fact, the number of community members grew to be what was believed to be the largest crowd ever to be gathered at Norton Field. It was believed, after a check at the main entrance of the field, that over 30,000 persons entered Norton in their cars while another 3,000 came by foot.[140] The large Ford Tri-Motor carried 352 persons over the city on Friday, followed by 392 passengers on Saturday and a record number of 475 individuals Sunday.[141]

Robert F. Kirk

Photo of "Columbus" Transcontinental Air Transport
(T.A.T.) plane christened at Norton Field, November, 1928.
(Notice the austere surroundings of Norton Field.)
Columbus Dispatch, November, 1928.
Photo courtesy of Columbus Dispatch.

The Building of an Airport: Port Columbus

It was a huge event with thousands of Columbus citizens coming for rides in the Ford Tri-Motor or to see the other aircraft that came for demonstrations and for displays. There were Ryan monoplanes, like the "Spirit", visiting for the event as well as a formation of five aircraft from the 112th Observation Squadron stationed at Cleveland.

Traffic was jammed on all major streets in the area including Broad Street during most of the afternoon as large crowds came to visit the event.

As the excitement rose concerning the bond issue and the building of a new municipal airport, Major Thomas Lanphier, Vice-President in charge of T.A.T. operations, provided more reasons to be in favor of the bond issue and the airport. He believed there would be an explosion of shops and factories building airplane accessories in Columbus should the municipal airport bond issue pass in November. "T.A.T. the line that plans to make Columbus the eastern air terminus…will begin operations in April…and the airport should be ready by that time. One plane a day each way will start the service, but in all probability would warrant an hourly schedule later."[142]

Thomas C. McMahon, Chief of the Technical Data Service, Army Air Corps, provided more information concerning the suitability of Columbus as an eastern terminus for T.A.T. He said, "Columbus is out of the storm area and on the edge of the hilly country which makes flying less safe to the east. It is the farthest eastern city in the level storm free area and is a…natural choice of engineers as an eastern terminus of airlines… an eastern center for manufacturing and an easy distribution point for finished products. May be one of the greatest terminals in the world."[143]

Meanwhile, Councilman Floyd Green, Chairman of the city Airport Commission, made a plea for support of the bond issue and the association went on record in a formal resolution as being in favor of the project.[144]

T.A.T continued to move forward with its projected plans. "The T.A.T. line… has ordered ten Ford-Stout all metal Tri-Motor monoplanes, carrying fourteen passengers in addition to pilot and mechanic. The largest single order for airplane equipment …has been placed with the Ford-Stout Airplane Company by T.A.T.," stated Major Thomas Lanphier.[145]

It can't be over emphasized the important and powerful role that Charles A. Lindbergh played in the advancement of aviation in America and in particular the advancement made in Columbus. "The non-stop flight of Charles A. Lindbergh from New York to Paris in 1927, perhaps more than any other single event, launched Columbus into the role of air pioneer. Following Lindbergh's triumphal visit here in 1928, inspired voters provided an $850,000 bond issue for the construction of Port Columbus."[146]

It was these inspired voters that were going to make the decision if the bond issue was to pass and thus provide Columbus with needed funding to build a new modern airport for the future.

"Whether or not Columbus is to have an airport and assume its rightful place...for aviation in America now is squarely up to the citizens of the city. Council has passed an ordinance submitting an $850,000 bond issue to the voters and will be placed on the ballots of the November election at the request of the Airport Commission. ...the sum is great enough to insure a part of 1,000 acres, fully equipped with all modern devices and facilities for handling the large fleets of planes."[147]

The Aviation Committee had done its work and investigated what kind of airport should be developed, including size, location and how it should be constructed. It not only looked to the needs of current demands but also looked to future demands that might present themselves. The Airport Committee had worked hard and developed a vision of the new airport and how much funding was necessary to see it become a reality.

CASTO'S "AMERICA'S GREATEST AIR HARBOR"

One of the first members of the Airport Commission was Don M. Casto Sr. He was a real estate broker and construction developer who had made a name for himself by establishing the city's first regional shopping centers. He found that as he built homes in new areas of town that housewives were reluctant to purchase a home far away from centers of commerce that included food stores, banks, post offices, etc. After noticing this problem Casto started building small but efficient shopping centers next to his housing developments. The housewives loved the concept and families then started purchasing homes in Casto's developments. The concept of integrating housing development with shopping centers nearby became a national phenomenon.[148]

Casto believed in the future of business aviation for Columbus as much as he believed in regional shopping opportunities. He believed that large cities in the country that had ocean or river access gave them special opportunities for commerce and trade. Columbus was landlocked and didn't have that opportunity for trade and commerce. However, he believed that what Columbus did have was a river of air that surrounded it. If Columbus took advantage of this river of air it could become a "Port" of trade and commerce like cities such as New York City. He coined the term "Port Columbus" to signify his belief in this concept. The term caught on and the name of the new future airport at Columbus was named "Port Columbus."

Casto wanted very much to see the 1928 Bond Issue pass to build a new airport.

He believed in promoting ideas to get them to sell. This was one of his strong points of leadership.

Casto's ideas of an Air Harbor and the importance of building the new airport were illustrated by two drawings that were published in the Dispatch.

Ad Advertising Port Columbus as an Air Harbor.
Columbus Dispatch, November 1, 1928.
Courtesy of Columbus Dispatch.

The Building of an Airport: Port Columbus

A Message –

To My Fellow Citizens of Columbus Upon My Departure For Germany Aboard the Graf Zeppelin

Air travel has come to stay. It has reached a practical stage. Moreover, with the increasing necessity for speeding up business, it is becoming more and more a necessary adjunct to the commercial life of the Nation.

I have left Lakehurst, N. J., aboard the Graf Zeppelin for Germany on business. I trust my next trip to Europe will be made direct from the "PORT OF COLUMBUS."

Columbus can never be a sea nor a lake port, but it can become a great airport---if Columbus voters so will it at the polls next Tuesday. Columbus' air advantages are superior to that of any Ohio city. We are on the direct transcontinental airway---the shortest line between the great cities of the East and the great cities of the West.

Western air travel is our right by reason of our fortunate location on the map. Also it will be logical to transfer Western travel to Europe aboard Zeppelins of the future at the "Port of Columbus" without the necessity of another transfer at Lakewood or New York. But a suitable airport must be provided by the citizens of Columbus if this is to become a reality.

New York seized its opportunity as a water port and the world's greatest city has been the result. Other cities, like Cleveland and Buffalo, have profited by lake transportation facilities to become great cities. The airways are the transportation highways of the future. Columbus should seize its golden opportunity to take a big forward stride as one of the important cities of America and vote for the airport bond issue at the polls next Tuesday.

Vote for the Airport November 6th

A message from Don Casto to Columbus Citizens, Vote for the Bond Issue!
Columbus Dispatch, October 29, 1928.
Courtesy of Columbus Dispatch.

One of Casto's missions had been going to Europe on the Graf Zeppelin to visit established airports in Germany and France and to collect information on their operations. His mission was to collect "Valuable data concerning construction, maintenance and operation of airports, secured at some of Europe's most famous flying fields...turn it over to city engineers and members of the airport commission."[149]

This is exactly what he did while in Europe. He contacted notable figures in German and French aviation and secured invaluable information in the laying out and constructing of a new and modern airport.[150] He visited Berlin, Paris and Cologne and interviewed experts at airports there. Experts at these locations gave him extremely valuable information that he was able to bring back and share with Columbus officials.

Casto was greatly impressed with the progress that Germany and France had made in aviation and in the building of their airports. He wrote of one airport, "...resembles an immense railway terminal, with an administration building larger than our own Union Station. In this administration building are large waiting rooms, smoking rooms, restaurants, barber shops, beauty parlors and all the stores and shops found in our busy railway terminals."[151]

He talked about the control towers of the large airports and how they were located in prominent positions with traffic managers who signaled and controlled all incoming and departing air traffic as smoothly as clockwork.[152]

An interesting point of information relayed by Casto was that, "Safety and comfort of passengers is the first consideration...and one of the little precautions necessitates the location of a man on the field to observe the manner in which incoming pilots land. If the pilot makes a bumpy landing, he is credited with a demerit. Six demerits cost him a salary reduction, and you may be assured all landings are extremely good."[153]

Through Casto's efforts, operation, maintenance and construction figures were sent to Columbus for use by those in charge of construction of Port Columbus to benefit from all of the experience and years of operation of these European airports.

Some of the useful information that was relayed concerned the building of runways and the numerous experiments with turf on those airport surfaces.

The Building of an Airport: Port Columbus

The highlight of Casto's trip to Europe was his journey on the Graf Zeppelin. He had traveled on almost every means of transportation on his trip from Columbus to New York, flight to Germany on the Zeppelin and a return trip to the United States on the steamer Ile De France. He had traveled more than 10,000 miles in 20 days.[154] His trip on the Graf Zeppelin departed for Germany on October 29, 1928 and ended when the Zeppelin landed in Germany on November 1, 1928. The trip took a total of 4 days.

"Unanimous approval of the proposed municipal airport was given by Columbus Council following a report and recommendation of its Aviation Committee. Report of the Aviation Committee was submitted following investigation and visits to some of the largest airports in the United States. The committee visited fourteen of the largest airports in operation traveling over 11,000 miles during a period of fourteen weeks."[155]

The details of the new bond issue were published and the Aviation Committee was very smart in the way they promoted this bond. In the bond issue in 1927 too many items were placed on the ballot. With multiple items on the list the cost for the bond went sky-high. Each of the items on the bond probably would have helped the city and its citizens but not to the same degree. Though some people wanted one or two of the items, they rejected the others. With the total cost of the bond being so high the natural instinct was to vote it down.

THE MOMENTUM BUILDS FOR PORT COLUMBUS

This time with only the building of the airport on the bond, focus was made on the vital importance of this one item. The bond was also better explained on how it was to be paid for and what the great benefit would be to Columbus citizens.

The sum for the bond was $850,000 and the "Maximum number of years which the bonds shall run is 22 years. The airport is the only bond issue to be submitted to the people November 6, 1928 and that is the proposed Columbus Municipal Airport… a vote for the bond issue means more factories, more employment and more wages for Columbus working people."[156]

Robert F. Kirk

Union Ad in support of airport bond issue.
Columbus Dispatch, November 4, 1928.
Courtesy of Columbus Dispatch.

The Building of an Airport: Port Columbus

The Columbus Dispatch published a large article that did a great job of explaining to the people how and why they should vote for the bond issue.

Items stated in the article included:

"Why?	In order that Columbus may share in the commercial and industrial advantages growing out of aviation.

Where located?	By Army Reserve Depot, bound on the north and west by James Pike, on the east by Poth Road and on south by the B. & O and Pennsylvania tracks – 15 minutes from Broad and High.

How selected?	Members of Columbus Airport Commission created by Council and appointed by Mayor Thomas. After consultation with Colonel Lindbergh, Ford Engineers, expert pilots and aviation authorities.

Why this site?	Minimum investment by the city, closest available acreage to Broad and High Streets, isolated from residential developments, railroad facilities for both freight and passenger use, and character of the ground.

Price?	- $850,000.
Size?	-Approximately - 1,000 acres
Partial Cost:
Real Estate (Ground clearing)	- $330,000

<u>Equipment, Structure and Drainage</u>	- $250,000;
<u>Cost of Runways and Roads, Leveling Ground, Seeding Field, Lighting, etc.</u>	- $270,000.
<u>Plan to Start</u>	- Early Spring, 1929"[157]

One issue that came to the surface of the bond issue and building of an airport was that of flying safety. Citizens had come a long way toward building confidence in the airplane as a safe mode of transportation. But still, some were not convinced. So some information was published in the Columbus Dispatch aimed at helping people feel a little better about the safety of flight.

The approach was to compare airplane travel to that of train travel. The railroads had long overcome the fear of those who would ride as passengers. In the beginning of rail travel passengers were afraid of what might happen if the boiler exploded on the engine. "At one time railway companies were required…to place a car loaded with sand bags between the locomotive and the passengers for when and if the boilers exploded," said I.C. McMahon, Chief of Materials Division of the U.S. Army Air Corps.[158] He went on to say, "Fear of air travel is not greater than fear of rail travel was then, and it is slowly disappearing."[159] He continued, "The United States has an airway system which is the envy of the entire world, especially in the Air Mail Service."[160]

One interesting note is that the idea of delivering the Columbus Dispatch by airplane to distant locations within the state was discussed. The extended time it took to take the Dispatch by car to distant rural locations could be drastically reduced if newspaper bundles could be taken by air and dropped at predetermined locations and then delivered quickly to customers.

The Building of an Airport: Port Columbus

Questions and Answers Concerning Columbus New Airport.
Photo courtesy of Stork Collection. Stork _022

Robert F. Kirk

Dispatch Rural Routes to Be Covered by Airplanes

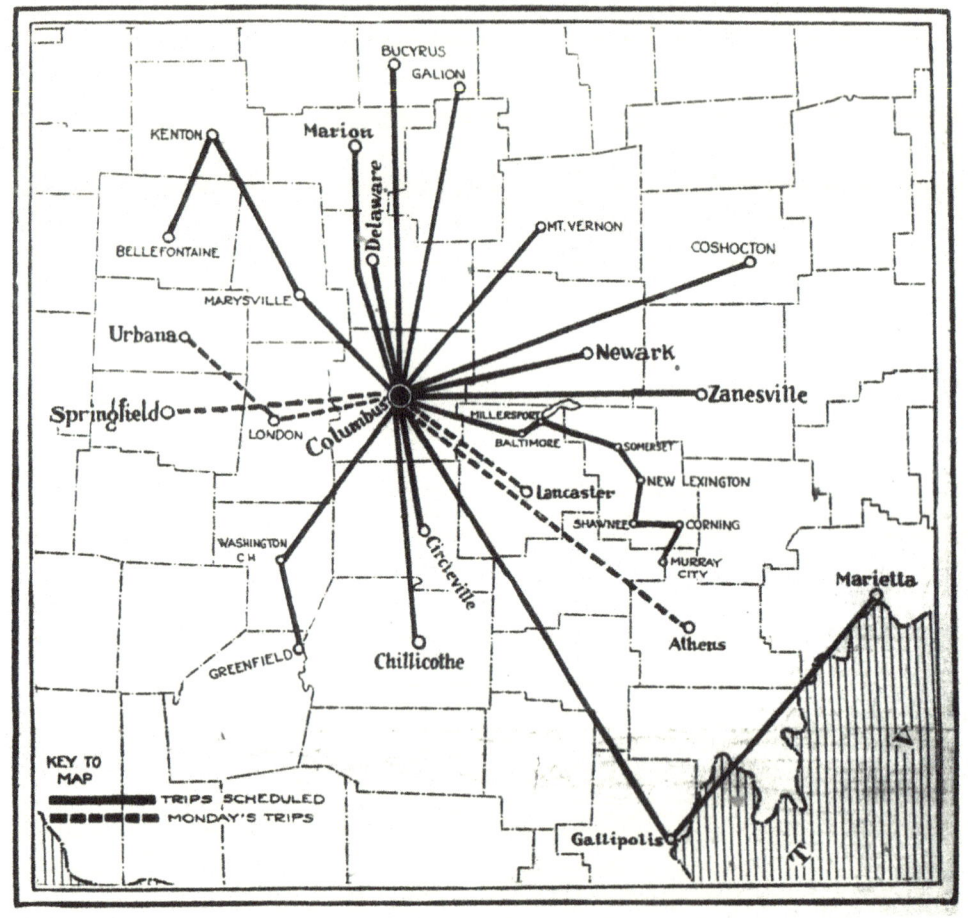

Drawing of Map showing Drop Zones for Air Delivered
Newspapers from Columbus Dispatch.
Columbus Sunday Dispatch, October 28, 1928.
Courtesy of Columbus Dispatch.

"To demonstrate the economic possibilities of the airplane in making time-limited shipments, The Dispatch has arranged to deliver copies of its editions to out-of-town subscribers via planes this week. The map above shows the routes to be covered by planes."[161]

The big day finally arrived and the bond issue vote was held on Tuesday, November 6, 1928. The report of the outcome was rapid and overwhelming. "Airport to be opened as soon as possible! With Columbus Airport bond issue approved by an overwhelming majority, city officials were ready to swing into action to carry out the mandate of voters at the earliest possible moment."[162]

THE BOND ISSUE PASSES: THE CITY MOVES!

The bond issue passed with a 5 to 1 majority. bond issue polled 87,445 yes votes, while 20,224 voters disapproved, giving the project a majority of 67,221 votes.[163]

Mayor James J. Thomas expressed the thoughts of so many that worked to pass the bond issue and move aviation forward in Columbus. "I regard this as one of the most important forward steps that Columbus voters have taken since I have been in office. With construction work to begin in the near future, I believe Columbus will reap a benefit greater than any of us realize, when the airport is in operation."[164]

The selection of the airport site, its purchase and the building and equipping of the new airport really turned out to be a great deal for the Columbus people as compared to that paid by other cities for their airports. Comparisons can be seen by the following costs:

Cleveland Airport – 1040 acres of land cost $1,250,000 for land alone; $400,000 more than the entire cost of the Columbus airport. It was located 7 miles from town.

St. Louis Airport – 693 acres of land cost $485,000 and spent $1,463,000 improving it. It was 14 miles from the city.

Newark Airport – 580 acres of land cost $4,500,000 and improvements cost $1,100,000. Total cost $5,600,000. It was only two miles from the city. The cost of Newark was more than 5 times that of Port Columbus with only about half the land.

Buffalo Airport – 518 acres of land cost $411,000 and improvements cost $391,000. The airport was 10 miles from business district and not near as complete as Port Columbus.[165]

The influence and guidance placed on this major project was illustrated by comments made by T.A.T.'s leaders. "The airport site has the approval of America's foremost aviation experts, including Colonel Charles A. Lindbergh, Major Thomas Lanphier, Colonel Paul Henderson, Charles 'Casey' Jones, and numerous others, all of whom declare it is ideally situated and will provide Columbus with air facilities that will be unequaled in any other inland city."[166]

Ford Motor Company also was consulted by officials of the Airport Commission who went to Detroit to ask for assistance in the selection of the proposed airport site. "Because of the vast experience of the Ford Motor Company in the operation of heavy transport planes, officials of the Airport Commission went to Detroit and laid the plans for the Columbus Port before W. C. Mayo, Chief Engineer of the Ford Organization, T. F. Sultan, Airport Engineer of St. Louis and Wendell Miller, drainage engineer, were employed to make preliminary investigations which resulted in carefully prepared data on the ...practical operation with both light and heavy airplanes."[167]

"The site was now made the unanimous choice of the members of the Columbus Airport Commission, said Chairman Floyd F. Green. He went on to name the Members of the Commission: They included Mr. Green, Kline L. Roberts, Henry W. Worley, Clare E. Cook, Alex F. Hammond, B. G. Huntington, Malcolm D. Jeffery, Frank C. Karns, John A. Kelley, Robert Lazarus, Stanley M. Ross, John M. Vorys, Emile E. Watson, Edgar T. Wolfe and Don M. Casto."[168]

Amelia Earhart also stated her view of the passing of the bond issue and the importance of having a major airport in the city. "Columbus is to be congratulated upon passing a bond issue for a first-class airport," Miss Earhart said, "...and declared the city was ideally situated, geographically, to become one of the most important air centers in the middle-west. Any town that does not at least provide a landing field will be left entirely out of the picture in a few years."[169]

"T.A.T., the line which will make Columbus Airport its eastern air terminal, will dedicate the first of 10 ships to be placed in service on the line at Norton Field next week... It is to be christened 'Miss Columbus' according to plans announced in New York by T.A.T. officials."[170]

No sooner than the announcement was made another airline published that it was to begin air service out of the new Columbus Airport. "Universal Aviation Corporation, which will start a line from Columbus to Dallas, will use Fokker F-10 Tri-Motored monoplanes, seating 12 passengers. Two planes each way, each day will use the municipal airport."[171]

A First Citizens Trust Company ad in The Columbus Dispatch expressed bright hopes for the new airport's impact. "The vote for the airport definitely marks Columbus as a forward-looking city in which all industry may find encouragement and every necessary cooperation."[172]

The analogies between the great ocean harbors and the newly funded airport "Air Harbor" in Columbus continued to be made in the newspapers. "The shipping industry centered about New York because that metropolis has the finest harbor, the best access to the hinterland, the best facilities. Nature has provided Columbus with the best natural air harbor in the country. Railroad facilities here provide the necessary adjunct for successful commerce while Port Columbus, experts claim, will provide complete airport service in the United States. Air commerce will be attracted to the Columbus Air Harbor just as water commerce chose New York as its chief port."[173]

The bond issue for the funding of the new airport in Columbus was approved with an overwhelming majority. All knew early that the tide had turned in the community for support for the airport project. Because T.A.T. wanted to start its operation at least by the summer of 1929 plans began immediately to get the airport underway. One of the first things that had to be done was the surveying of the airport site to see what needed to be cleared and how drainage was to be set up for the airport. Work on the project actually began at least three weeks before the election.

Robert F. Kirk

An ad from Don Casto to Columbus Citizens, July 7, 1929
stating "Columbus, The Nation's Greatest Air Harbor".
Courtesy of Columbus Dispatch.

The Building of an Airport: Port Columbus

"The survey upon which a crew has been working for the past three weeks in anticipation of approval of the bond issue and the maps will be completed by Monday. Work will be started immediately upon the plans for draining the field."[174]

Photo of heavy piece of construction equipment used to clear the field.
Photo courtesy of Stork Collection: Stork _185

Photo of field of new airport as it is being cleared.
Photo courtesy of Stork Collection: Stork _164

To make sure that the city was ready to construct the new airport, plans were put in place to ensure the leaders were prepared and doing the right thing.

On February 4, 1929 the City Council authorized the appointment of a City Commission composed of a city executive and a member of the City Council to inspect selected airports in the middle-west and eastern sections of the United States.[175] Mayor Thomas represented the city and Floyd Green, Chairman of the Council Service Committee was appointed to represent the city's legislative body. The two city officials made plans and traveled to Cleveland, Chicago, Buffalo, Syracuse, Newark, and several other cities.[176] During their trip questions came up concerning runway construction. Several airport managers had differing ideas on what was best but the Columbus city leaders decided that concrete runways would be the best.[177]

The city leaders were proud of the results of their labors in passing the bond and selecting the field for the new airport. The 650-acre terminal represented a two-year fight for a port made by city officials, civic organizations, businessmen and others interested in the city's future. It also represented the final decision of more than 80,000 voters that Columbus should make a decisive bid to become the inland air capital of the United States.[178]

It had been decided early in the airport process that Columbus Airport was not going to be just a "...landing field. It will not be just a dismal stretch of land on which airplanes may alight, and taxi up to a barren hangar."[179] It had been determined that the new airport would be one of the best, or even perhaps, the best airport in the world.

"Tentative plans which have already been made will provide for this city an airport which will be better equipped to handle air traffic than Croydon in England, Le Bourget in France, or Templehof in Berlin," said Kline L. Roberts, Secretary of the Airport Commission.[180]

The visits of Don M. Casto and others to Europe to visit well-known airports provided models for Port Columbus' future. The European airports had large waiting rooms at the airports with reading rooms, clocks and timetables that would accurately depict the takeoffs and landings of the commercial planes. The planners at Port Columbus were not going to be out done. For them, "...Port Columbus will resemble a union station, with its ticket booths, waiting rooms, restaurant, promenade, and living quarters for pilots and other field attaches."[181]

Aircraft traffic was expected to be very active even from the airport opening and to grow in numbers very quickly. T.A.T. had two ships leaving for the west coast each day along with two flights each day leaving for Dallas, Texas. Those were large aircraft carrying at least 12 passengers. They were equipped with the best and most modern equipment. This included aircraft radios so there could be communication between other aircraft and communication with the ground stations. The ground stations relayed valuable information relating to bad or hazardous weather along with possible traffic delays.

The plans also called for the aircraft flying into and out of Port Columbus to be the most modern, safest and luxurious of any available. The T.A.T. aircraft had modern radios for communication, but it also had first class service with china serving dishes, fine silverware and cloth table coverings to be used on special aluminum serving tables. There was also an on board steward who provided magazines and hot sandwiches and coffee.[182]

It was decided that Port Columbus was to be one of the most beautiful airports in the world. Leaders wanted it to follow a general architectural design based on that of the administration-passenger plan.

City Service Director W. H. Duffy set in motion all of the resources of each individual city department and made every possible effort to make sure that the airport was completed by the time T.A.T. was ready to start their flights. These were planned to begin either in May or June, 1929.[183]

Service Director Duffy issued instructions for plans of the airport to be drawn by City Engineer Robert Simpson and H.M. Stork, draftsman.[184] In preparation for this assignment, "City Engineer Simpson had written to officials at Newark, N.J. for all data concerning plans, and operations of the proposed $6,000,000 airport being installed there, in order that he may have the benefit of findings of New Jersey engineers... Simpson received data on nearly all airports in the country...and will be ready to go to work on the project without delay, insuring speedy opening of the field."[185]

Robert F. Kirk

Photo of airport leaders from left to right, Centner, Stork, and Mayor Thomas with Erbeck from Western Electric.
Photo courtesy of Stork Collection: Stork _247

It was decided that there needed to be a new division in the city government to handle the affairs of the new airport. It was to be called the Division of Air Transportation. "A new branch of city government is to be established in Columbus. It will be known as the Division of Air Transportation and will be charged with the duty of operating the new municipal airport Columbus is to build."[186]

The Allied Architect Association of Columbus was commissioned to draw up plans and specifications for the Administration-Depot building with a cost of about $50,000.[187] Herbert Baumer was the architect. He was a professor at The Ohio State University and Chief Architect on several other projects. He studied in France and his philosophy of building was that the building and the site be indissoluble. The building and the site must fit together so there was no contrast between the building and its setting.[188]

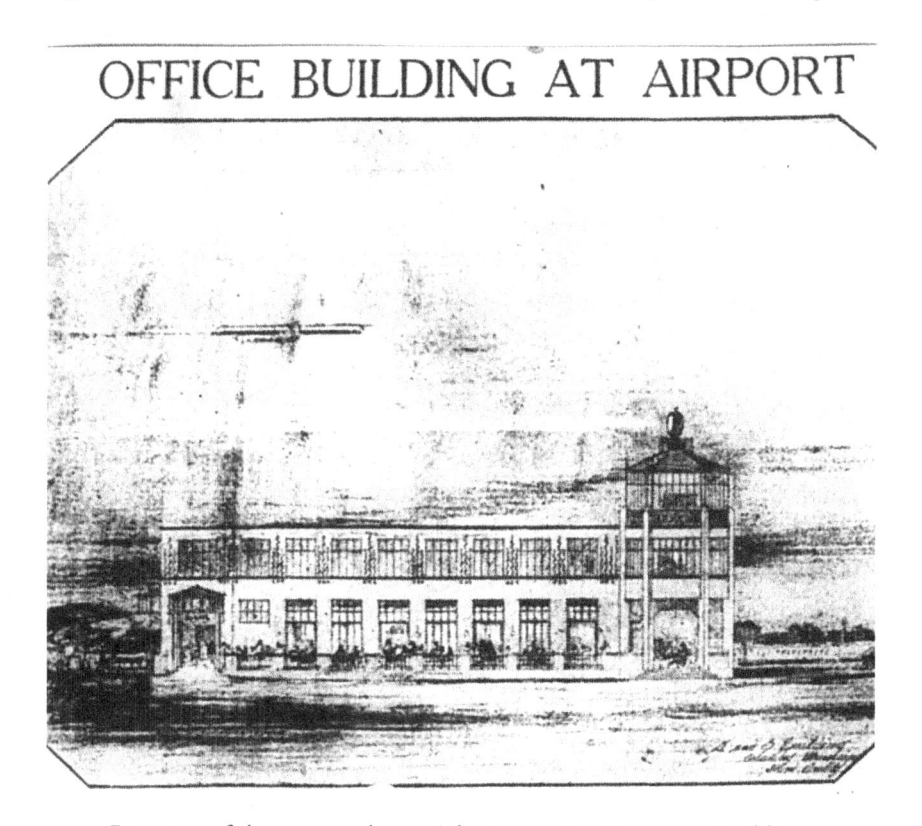

Drawing of the proposed new Administration-Passenger Building.
The Columbus Citizen, February 6, 1929.
Courtesy of Columbus Dispatch.

It should be noted that high priced airport engineers that layout airport designs at great costs offered to design and build Port Columbus but their offers were rejected.

C. R. Chappelear Company received the contract for the construction of the Administration-Passenger building.

To speed up the development of the new airport many pieces of the airport puzzle had to be put into place. The first of these was to procure the needed land. Some of the land could be purchased out right. This was the 360 acres of land for the initial construction of the airport proper. The other part would have to go through the condemnation process to provide a total of approximately 1000-acres. Floyd Green declared, "He was of the opinion that the city can procure several hundred acres of the 1000 acres proposed site without condemnation and especially a 400 acre parcel near the point where the Pennsylvania Railroad Station and the T.A.T. hangars will be built."[189]

"Council of Columbus will condemn, if necessary, the land needed for the municipal airport… Council decided to take this action in order to get construction started on the landing field yet this year. It is planned to use approximately 360 acres of land for the port."[190]

Don M. Casto, who was on the Air Board Commission, had worked very hard to promote the proposed new airport and had worked the system to get on the Graf Zeppelin and travel on the first Transatlantic eastbound trip from the United States to Europe on the Zeppelin. It was the first flight from the New World to the Old World. He did this to advertise the importance of modern air travel and to have a modern airport at Columbus.

He wrote, "We cannot fail to connect in a big way with air programs and developments which are today sweeping this country. So, we are building Great Airports, building up our Great Air Harbors; 'dredging our channels' and 'building our docks.' In the future our city will be literally circled by air transportation fields and centers of air industry… Through the unprecedented opportunity that nature has laid at our doorstep." He went on to say, "The Air, has come to Columbus…"[191]

The importance of the approved new airport at Columbus continued to be talked and written about. It was named, "America's Air Capital." It was really hard to believe that the new airport bond issue had been approved and now the "greatness" of the airport's reality became known as the "Truths of Columbus."

The advantages of the new airport's location was constantly advertised and discussed as listed below:

1. Columbus, because of its geographical location is the logical Gateway to the East and West.
2. Columbus, because of its climate and atmospheric conditions is for airport purposes, as nearly ideal as any spot in America.
3. Columbus, because of its topography of surrounding country offers ideal sites for additional landing fields and aircraft manufacturing plants.
4. Columbus is far enough from the seaboard to offer a safe location for the concentration of military aircraft and aircraft manufacturers.
5. Columbus, on Monday, will dedicate the most modernly equipped airport in America and the only one where rails and air transportation in reality meet.
6. No other city in America enjoys all the Geographical, Topographical, and Climatic advantages of Columbus."[192]

The Port was to be owned by the City of Columbus and operated by the municipality.

Airport personnel were to include:

"Manager
Assistant Manager in charge of maintenance and operations
Chief Clerk
Hangar Clerk
Several electricians
Ground Crew of 6
The Caretaker of the Administration Building

And there were other employees that made a total of approximately 50 persons."[193]

ERNEST H. STORK HELPS DESIGN AND BUILD PORT COLUMBUS

The responsibility to oversee and build the Port was placed under the supervision of the City Engineer, E. H. Stork.[194]

"Ernest H. Stork was delegated by city officials and the Airport Committee to take charge of laying out and the construction of the new $850,000 municipal airport. Stork is a draftsman in the City Engineering Department and laid out air fields in France during the war."[195] "This experience in France was the background fitting Stork for the place of consulting engineer in building the city's airport."[196]

Stork had served in the U.S. military and with a rank of sergeant operated as a master signal electrician. He was married and had a son and a daughter.

Stork became known as the "Designer of Port Columbus."[197]

"Ernest H. Stork, who designed and superintended the construction of Port Columbus was promoted yesterday to the grade of assistant engineer in the city division of engineering."[198]

Stork moved up through the ranks at the city and the airport and went from draftsman, assistant engineer, engineer and Assistant Superintendent of Port Columbus.

He wore several hats while working for the city including that of acting secretary of the city planning commission.[199]

Stork had been working on the plans for the municipal airport since before the passage of the bond issue in November.[200]

The plans were to have Port Columbus ready for use by May 1, 1929. It was understood for this goal to take place, to go from start and build a complete new airport and have it ready to use in just 6 months was an ambitious endeavor. To do so we, "…must work every minute to get it done and may employ 500 men to build the airport."[201]

Photo of Captain William Centner, first Superintendent of Port
Columbus and Ernest Stork, Assistant Superintendent.
Photo courtesy of Stork Collection: Stork _062

The Building of an Airport: Port Columbus

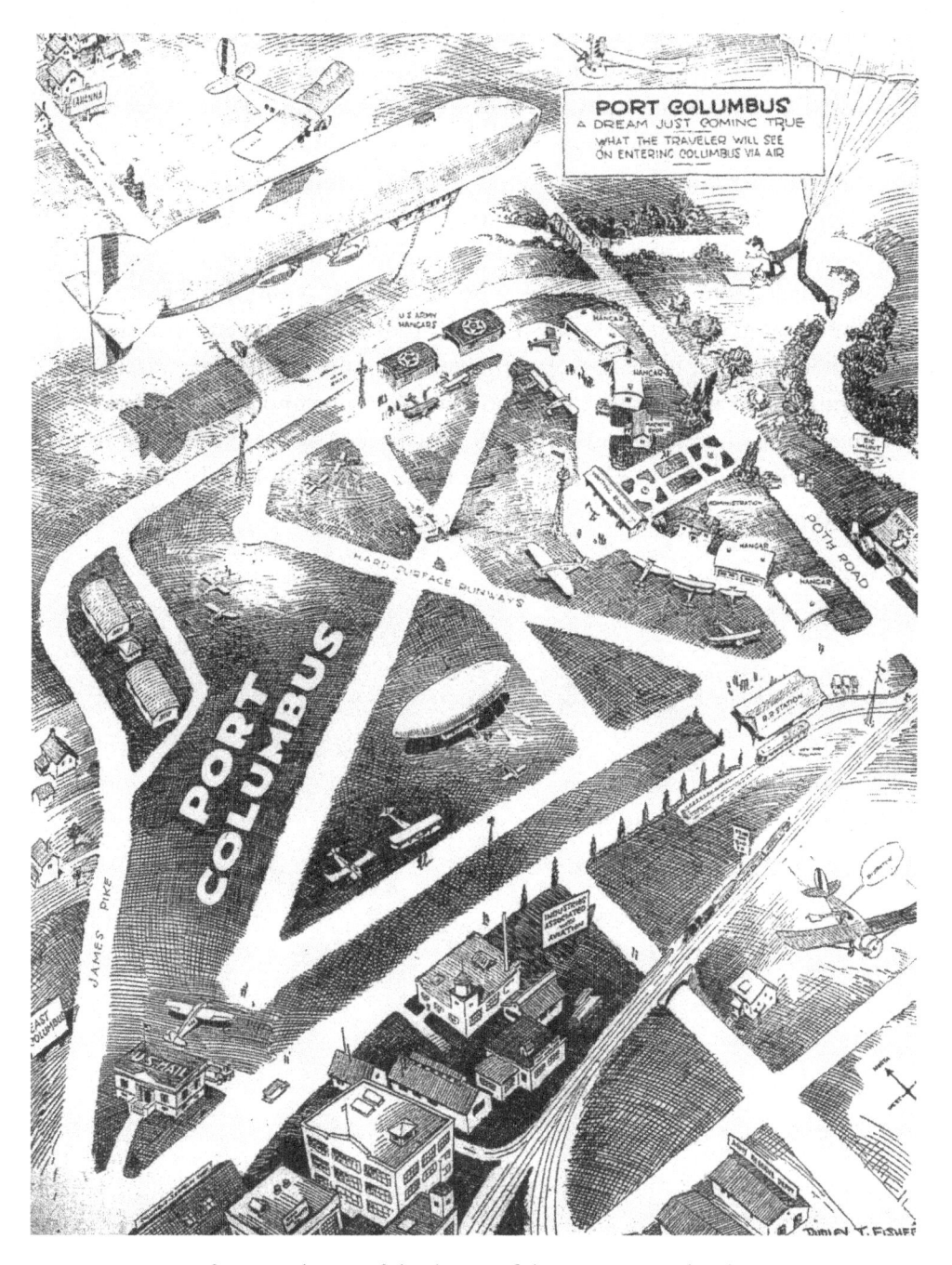

Drawing of artistic dream of the design of the new Port Columbus Airport.
Columbus Dispatch, November 9, 1928.
Courtesy of Columbus Dispatch.

The design of Port Columbus was developed and showed where the different structures including the runways would be placed. "A model was produced by Allied Architects Association and is an exact picture of the new municipal airport. At the right of the picture are the administration buildings, signal tower and field offices, behind the concrete 'apron' that borders the landing field…Pennsylvania railroad lines touch the corner of the Port, and their switches for transfer of passengers from trains to airplanes on the first transcontinental route… The diagonal white lines are the 100-foot wide concrete runways, which will enable planes of any size… to take off in any weather regardless of mud or snow. At the lower left…is ample space for the erection of aircraft factories that the new Port is expected to attract to Columbus. Around the borders of the field…provisions have been made for construction of hangars…"[202]

The Building of an Airport: Port Columbus

Photo of Columbus Mayor James J. Thomas with a trowel, helping lay the cornerstone at the Administration-Passenger building at Port Columbus airport, April 18, 1929. The cornerstone reads "Port Columbus Administration Station."
Columbus Dispatch, April 1929.
Photo courtesy of Columbus Dispatch.

Robert F. Kirk

Photo of construction of Administration-Passenger Building and T.A.T. Hangar following the plan of the Allied Architects' Model. Photo courtesy of Chuck Blardone Collection.

"The design of the new Administration-Passenger Building was prepared by the Allied Architects' Association, with a cost of the new structure estimated at $50,000."[203]

It was decided that the Administration-Passenger Building, along with the hangars, would be constructed out of concrete and brick. Buff colored bricks with black strips and slate trim would be the colors.[204] The combined administration and passenger building was 106 feet long, 34 feet wide and was two stories high with an additional basement.[205]

"At the northwest corner is an octagonal tower whose diameter is 20 feet. This is a glass- enclosed tower that provides a clear view of all parts of the field."[206]

Inside the tower was located the airport weather bureau and the lighting control switchboard. The tower controller could turn on or off any light on the field with the switches available in the tower.

"The first floor will contain the baggage and ticket offices, women's room, emergency hospital, pilot's lunchroom, kitchen, cashier, storage room, supply room, waiting room, dining room, telephones, information booth and newsstand. The second floor will have a women's room, men's room, showers, dressing room, pilot's lounge, offices, manager's office and T.A.T. Headquarters. A room is also available for the Department of Commerce representative who frequently visits the field.

The tower at the right-hand corner will house the control lights, operated from the manager's office, which will be enclosed in glass."[207] Postal and Western Union Telegraph Offices are also planned to be located in the Administration-Passenger Building.

"The present administration building is but a portion of that which eventually will be required. The future first annex will be at the western end, so that the octagonal tower will be in the center of the structure… There is ample space for other additions south of the present building."[208]

There was also a basement that provided space for the boiler room, power distribution room, the scullery, public comfort stations and a storage room.[209]

There was a weight scale for passengers and baggage in the Administration-Passenger Building. "So as the traveler steps upon a slightly elevated stage – really a scales platform – his weight and that of his baggage are automatically recorded, without his knowing it."[210]

Multiple telescoping sections of walkway canopies were available to be extended from the Administration-Passenger building to the covered train terminal to the south as well to the north to the awaiting Ford Tri-Motor aircraft. This helped shield passengers from inclement weather as well as keep them from dangerous moving propellers.[211]

Photo of telescoping walkway canopies without complete canvas covering. Photo courtesy of Ohio History Connection- Image #P245_B01F01_003

Also located in the Administration-Passenger Building was a Port Restaurant. It was operated by Miss Hazel Brown, who was a well-known "restaurateur." Passengers who stopped by to eat at the restaurant remarked that the food was good.

The Building of an Airport: Port Columbus

Photo of Port Columbus Restaurant's Advertisement.
Photo courtesy of Stork Collection: Stork _265

Robert F. Kirk

"—the dining salon in the administration building, modern to the minute, offering delicious food and efficient service."

Photo of Port Columbus Restaurant's Dining Area.
Photo courtesy of Ohio History Connection – Image #MSS454_B02_P.

T.A.T. AND PENNSYLVANIA RAILROAD ARE "ALL IN"

The location of the new Columbus Airport was selected and movement to secure the land moved forward with much success. The new airport "...will be located on acreage north of B & O and Pennsylvania railroad tracks and south of the James Pike from the point where it passes the army reserve depot to the juncture on Bagshaw Road and then on a line securing approximately 1000 acres of level land situated at a convenient distance from the center of the city with terrain capable of proper drainage and soil treatment without excessive cost and obtainable at a reasonable price."[212] The airport site near the Army Depot was chosen on the approval of Charles Lindbergh and other experts.[213]

The Pennsylvania Railroad Company agreed to build a passenger terminal on its tracks on the southeast corner of the new airport. It was agreed that it was to be located by the new Administration-Passenger Building, also on the southeast edge of the recently purchased land for the new airport.

The Pennsylvania Railroad passenger terminal design was, "Two concrete covered train sheds, 600 feet long, were built opposite the Port's administration-depot building. The city will erect a covered walk approximately 250 feet from these sheds to the waiting room entrance of the building."[214]

Robert F. Kirk

The Train Station at Port Columbus—Air Lines Can Learn from the Railroads

Photo of Pennsylvania Railroad Passenger Terminal.
Photo courtesy of Stork Collection: Stork _239

The Building of an Airport: Port Columbus

Photo of aerial view of Administration-Passenger Building (bottom left) and Pennsylvania Railroad Terminal with train (bottom center) and the T.A.T. hangar (middle right of photo). Drainage lines for airport can be seen between the two runways at upper middle of photo.
Photo courtesy of Stork Collection: _273

Robert F. Kirk

"Transcontinental Air Transport let the contract for their hangar, which cost approximately $100,000 to the Middle States Construction Company, which will receive the contract for the construction of the Curtiss Flying Service hangar,"[215]

T.A.T. built a construction headquarters to help in the many operations that were taking place concerning T.A.T and the construction of their sections of the airport.

Photo of T.A.T. construction headquarters.
Photo courtesy of Stork Collection: Stork _197

The Curtiss Flying Service hangar was the next one built on the east side of the airport next to the T.A.T hangar.

The T.A.T. hangar at Port Columbus, which was 206 feet by 145 feet and 22 feet high, was completed above the foundation in 50 working days. An incredible feat! The new hangar could hold six to nine Ford Tri-Motor aircraft.[216]

The Building of an Airport: Port Columbus

Photo of T.A.T. Hangar as it exists today at Port Columbus.
Photo by the author.

There were nine hangar spaces designed on the east side of Port Columbus by the Administration-Passenger Building that had been spoken for. The first one was the T.A.T. Hangar on Site No. 1. Site No. 2 was also reserved by T.A.T. even though they never built on it.

The third site was taken by the Curtiss Flying Service which started and completed its construction soon after Port Columbus opened.

The next hangar site was reserved by the city of Columbus to build a municipal hangar. Work on it started just after Port Columbus was opened and the cost for it reached a total of $110,000.[217] It had a different westerly design without the two story offices on the corners.

The same typical architectural design was adopted and used for all three of the first hangars.[218] In all, seven of the nine spaces had been reserved for building but only three were built before WW II.

The following photos show the progress made in the construction of the Port Columbus Hangar.

Robert F. Kirk

Photo of progress made on a regular basis constructing the Port Columbus Airport Hangar. The boiler is shown being installed.
Photo courtesy of Stork Collection: Stork _204

The Building of an Airport: Port Columbus

Photo of progress made on a regular basis constructing the Port Columbus Airport Hangar. Main rafter of the roof is being put in place.
Photo courtesy of Stork Collection: Stork _205

Photo of progress made on a regular basis constructing the Port Columbus Airport Hangar. Main roof rafter has been attached to vertical I-beams.
Photo courtesy of Stork Collection: Stork _207

Robert F. Kirk

Photo of progress made on a regular basis constructing the Port Columbus Airport Hangar. Progress being made on roof construction.
Photo courtesy of Stork Collection: Stork _211

Photo of progress made on a regular basis constructing the Port Columbus Airport Hangar. All main roof rafters have been put in place.
Photo courtesy of Stork Collection: Stork _212

The Building of an Airport: Port Columbus

Photo of progress made on a regular basis constructing
the Port Columbus Airport Hangar.
Photo courtesy of Stork Collection: Stork _214

Photo of progress made on a regular basis constructing the Port
Columbus Airport Hangar. Installing the roof over the roof rafters.
Photo courtesy of Stork Collection: Stork _216

Photo of progress made on a regular basis constructing the Port Columbus Airport Hangar. Concrete interior flooring is being installed.
Photo courtesy of Stork Collection: Stork _217

Photo of progress made on a regular basis constructing the Port Columbus Airport Hangar. Interior concrete flooring is completed with roof about half complete.
Photo courtesy of Stork Collection: Stork _219

The Building of an Airport: Port Columbus

Photo of progress made on a regular basis constructing the Port Columbus Airport Hangar. Construction begins on brick sidewalls.
Photo courtesy of Stork Collection: Stork _220

Photo of progress made on a regular basis constructing the Port Columbus Airport Hangar. Roof and sidewall about completed.
Photo courtesy of Stork Collection: Stork _222

Photo of completed T.A.T. hangar.
Photo courtesy of Stork Collection: Stork _237

One mile north of the field T.A.T. built a radio station with two tall towers that it designed to communicate with ground to ground stations, ground to air stations and even to multiple stations along the T.A.T. route.[219] The radio stations were able to be in contact with the T.A.T. weather station on the Port Columbus field at the Administration-Passenger building and the T.A.T. hangar. The weather that was collected and analyzed by meteorologists at the T.A.T. offices at Port Columbus made the weather conditions available to all arriving and departing T.A.T. aircraft at the airport.

The Building of an Airport: Port Columbus

Photo of T.A.T. Radio Station along the Albuquerque Air Route.
Photo courtesy of Stork Collection: Stork _154

Robert F. Kirk

Photo inside the T.A.T. Radio Building.
Photo courtesy of Stork Collection: Stork _155

The Building of an Airport: Port Columbus

Photo of electrical generators in basement of T.A.T. Radio Station.
Photo courtesy of Stork Collection: Stork _264

After the bond was passed in 1928, the first task was to get the ownership of the newly acquired airport land under the ownership of the city. The new airport became a municipal field owned and operated by the city. The land selected by Lindbergh and the Airport Commission was east of the city and just one half mile north of Norton Field. The total amount of land decided on was 1,000 acres, but only 360 acres was initially purchased so the development could begin. Steps were taken by the legal department either to purchase or condemn the land. Pending receipt of the money from the sale of the bonds, the city auditor loaned other municipal money to purchase the land, and reimbursement was to take place when the bonds were sold.[220]

Earnest H. Stork had been placed in charge of the development of the new airport as well as its design. He was also named as Assistant Manager of the airport while William F. Centner was named the Superintendent of the Airport.[221]

Stork, had gained experience laying out airports while serving in the U.S. Army during WW I in France and that experience served him well working on the Port Columbus Airport.

CONSTRUCTION BEGINS

Drainage

"The first step...in anticipation that the bonds would pass at the November election held in 1928...Professor Frank Eno of Ohio State University, a man prominent in soil study was given free rein to investigate the earth taken from the field for drainage purposes."[222]

Stork and Eno worked together and took boring samples from the field to study soil composition. The results of their tests showed that a very extensive drainage system was needed to drain the airport properly. The earth samples showed a dense clay material that was not good for easy water drainage. Percolation tests were accomplished to gain information on the kind of drainage material and efficiency needed to properly drain the field.[223]

It became apparent from the study that what was needed was a series of drain lines dug into the soil that required being lined with drainage tiles, surrounded by pea gravel. On top of this, larger coarse gravel would be filled within eight inches of the surface. The water then could drain through the thin soil, through the coarse and pea gravel into the tile pipes and drained off the property.

Several types of tile were tested for strength, material and price. Common clay farm drain tile was eliminated because of the great stress induced by large commercial aircraft landing on them and crushing the tile. Corrugated steel pipe was also looked at but it was too expensive to be used. After much testing and cost analysis it was decided that Vitrified Shale Tile was the best choice. It was manufactured within a mile of the airport thus making it very economical for purchase and use.

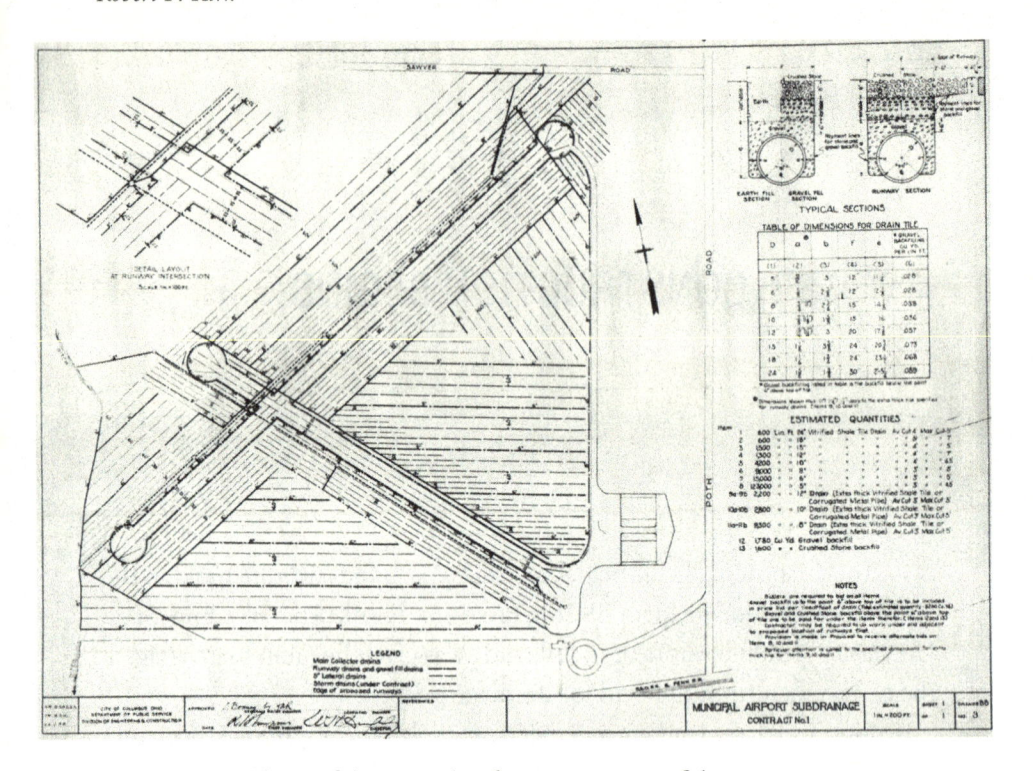

Photo of drawing plan for construction of drainage
system for Port Columbus Airport.
Photo courtesy of Stork Collection: Stork _328

However, before Vitrified Shale Tile was selected it had to pass the stress tests that all tiles considered for use had to undergo. Stork and his men conducted exhaustive tests of all tiles before selecting one.

"Two test pits were dug three feet square by about four feet deep, about 30 feet apart, the tile was placed at a depth it would be laid at the airport between the two pits, and being surrounded by the porous material and backfill soil. Tamped into place."[224] Then the tests began. A large truck was loaded with fifteen tons of rock or gravel to be used for the test. The heavy truck was driven over the test tile areas and checked to see the results on the tested tile. If the tile passed this test then a drop test was done to see if the tile tested could withstand the weight of a fully loaded transport plane landing on top of the tile trench.

"While watching the test through the two test pits, the fifteen ton trucks were driven over an eight inch railroad tie that had been placed next

The Building of an Airport: Port Columbus

to the tile trench. The truck, running over the railroad tie then dropped onto the tile trench from a height of 8 inches. This placed tremendous weight and stress on the tile at the bottom of the test trench. The weight was very similar to that of a fully loaded transport plane landing on the field. The Vitrified Shale Tile was depressed but it was found that it had withstood the impact of the truck's weight."[225]

Exhaustive tests on different tiles were also made to determine which ones could withstand the most pounds of weight before they were broken or crushed. The results of the tests showed that the Vitrified Tile withstood up to 2,260 pounds before it broke, while other tiles broke at 800 to 900 pounds. This test along with the truck drop test showed that the Vitrified Tile was the best selection for the airport. It withstood the force of landing transport aircraft best without being crushed or broken. [226]

To make sure that the new airport was drained properly and that there would be no problem with the collection of water on the runways or even in the grass areas of the field a very large and well-designed drainage plan was put into place.

"Outside of the runway areas, rows of tile are spaced 60-ft apart with a minimum covering of two feet of dirt. On areas 200-ft each side of the runways, spacing is 30 ft.

In all, there is 163,000 ft. of drain tile in the area."[227] This translated to 32 miles of drain tile under the surface of the airport.[228]

This massive drainage effort was required by the Department of Commerce to make sure that the airport had super-drained areas.

To make this great drainage distance possible, large mechanized "Buckeyes", or trench diggers, were used to dig the great distance of trenches. These Buckeyes could dig several feet of trench at the rate of 12 feet per minute.[229]

Robert F. Kirk

Vitrified Bedford Shale Drain Tile Stand The Test

Extract From Columbus Dispatch, Jan. 18, 1929

They Cost no More

Why Not Buy The Best

Exhaustive tests of tile submitted for use on the new municipal airport were conducted by the city engineering department during the past week.

Trenches were dug at the new city material yard, West Spring street, to the depth that will be necessary on the airport, varying from 12 to 36 inches. The tile was placed in the trenches and covered over, and a huge truck, filled with gravel, run over an obstruction and allowed to drop from varying heights on top of the trenches.

This simulated the impact of landing of a huge transport plane. Observation pits were dug at each end of the trenches, in order that effect of the impact might be observed. The truck weighed 13¾ tons, loaded, and impact sustained by the tile was much greater than would occur in actual use on the airport.

In the photograph above, the truck is seen running over a seven-inch obstruction, allowing the weight to drop from that height to the trench beneath.

Real Tile

Real Service

Make Satisfied Customers

Not a single piece of Bedford Shale tile was cracked or broken. And as a result of this test more than 200,000 feet of this high grade material was specified and is being used to drain the

Municipal Airport at Columbus, Ohio

which will be the eastern terminus of the Trans-Continental Airline and one of the most modern ports in the world.

Think what these tests mean to you in years of service or under extreme conditions. When you use Vitrified Bedford Shale tile the job is permanent.

Photo of fifteen ton test truck dropping down 8
inches on tile test trench at Port Columbus.
Photo courtesy of Stork Collection: Stork _316

Photo of large Buckeye trench digger working at Port Columbus. Photo courtesy of Stork Collection: Stork _174

"The main trunk of the storm sewer was next to start operations, beginning at the northeast corner of the field and at a depth of 16 feet. This four-foot reinforced concrete line was along the path of what was to be the main runways of the port. Just as soon as start was made on this project the lateral drains were started. These laterals consisted of small tile already mentioned in the test."[230]

To aid in the removal of excess amounts of water from the field the natural drainage was changed from west to northeast[231] so the water runoff could be carried away quickly and into Big Walnut Creek, a small stream adjacent to the airport.[232] The result of these efforts culminated in a storm sewer system that was 6,600 feet long, starting at 15 inches in diameter and increasing to 48 inches in diameter and carried all the water off the surface area of Port Columbus to Big Walnut Creek.[233]

This massive amount of work accomplished on the drainage system at Port Columbus resulted in the finest drainage system of any airport in the world.[234] The clay soil presented a large drainage problem but was overcome by subsoil tiling and sewage super draining. Approximately $78,000 was spent in overcoming the drainage problem. The result was an assurance that the "Harbor" could be used in any kind of weather.[235]

Robert F. Kirk

Photo of truck loading airport tile at Port Columbus.
Photo courtesy of Stork Collection: Stork _167

Photo of truck unloading airport tile.
Photo courtesy of Stork Collection: Stork _169

Photo of Buckeye digging trench and tile being laid by construction workers.
Photo courtesy of Stork Collection: Stork _175

Photo of Vitrified Tile being laid out by Buckeye and men.
Photo courtesy of Stork Collection: Stork _173

The Building of an Airport: Port Columbus

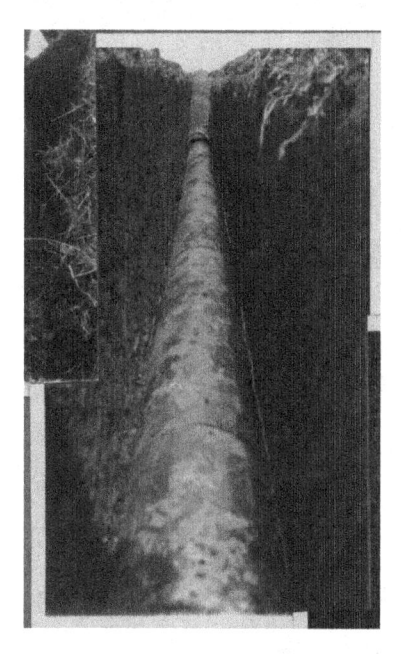

Photo of Vitrified Tile being laid with gravel at far end of trench.
Photo courtesy of Stork Collection: Stork _183

Photo of gravel being poured on top of Vitrified Tile.
Photo courtesy of Stork Collection: Stork _186

Photo of larger gravel being poured on top of smaller gravel.
Photo courtesy of Stork Collection: Stork _187

The Building of an Airport: Port Columbus

Photo of large area showing drainage tiles being installed at Port Columbus.
Photo courtesy of Stork Collection: Stork _196

Robert F. Kirk

Photo of large area showing drainage tiles being installed.
Photo courtesy of Stork Collection: Stork _103

The Building of an Airport: Port Columbus

Photo of truck with substantial tile pipe to be used for large flow drainage.
Photo courtesy of Stork Collection: Stork _170

Robert F. Kirk

Photo of substantial size reinforced concrete pipe
being unloaded for installation.
Photo courtesy of Stork Collection: Stork _191

The Building of an Airport: Port Columbus

Photo of large 48 inch reinforced concrete pipe being installed toward end of drainage system.
Photo courtesy of Stork Collection: Stork _193

Photo of end of storm drain system to deliver collected water to Big Walnut Creek reversing the natural drainage from west to northeast. Photo courtesy of Stork Collection: Stork _195 and _102

A contract to the B.F. Paterson Company was awarded in December 1928 for clearing the site which included about 600 trees ranging in diameter from small to 30 inch Elms or Pin Oaks.[236]

All of this work was done between November 1928 and March 1929. During April and May 1929, the grading of the field and the excavating for the runways began.[237]

There was only a difference of 20 feet in elevation across the airport field area. The highest point of elevation was 820 feet mean sea level (MSL) while the lowest point was 800 feet MSL. Thus making it easy to level and provide an almost perfect field for takeoffs and landings. The elevation difference was true for just about all of the 1,000 acres making up the airport.[238]

There was another advantage of this field that also helped in its selection. There were a number of ditches running through or next to the property that made it much easier to move the water rapidly off the field. "Two ditches are on the property and three-foot tile will be laid in them as the backbone of the drainage system. By taking advantage of the ditches, a savings of approximately $50,000 in the estimated drainage cost can be made, city engineers believe. Original estimates placed the drainage cost at $140,000."[239]

RUNWAY CONSTRUCTION BEGINS

As soon as the drainage project was completed the construction of the runways began. It was decided that for a start there would be two runways built. The longer "main" runway was 3500 feet long and oriented northeast to southwest. It was aligned to the prevailing southwest wind. The other runway was 2500 feet long and was oriented southeast to northwest. It was aligned to the northwestern direction of the strongest prevailing wind. Both runways were designed to be 100 feet wide. "In the final construction of the runways they were widened to be 200 feet wide. It has been recognized from the start, that in order to provide a field that will afford dependable service for the taking off and landing of heavy transport ships in all seasons, paved runways in at least two directions will be necessary; one in the direction of the prevailing wind, and the other, the high velocity winds."[240]

The two runways were connected by a 2000-foot taxiway. The runways had large turning circles at each end. The circles were called turning buttons. The taxiways were widened into a circle where planes could be turned around before takeoff or after landing.[241]

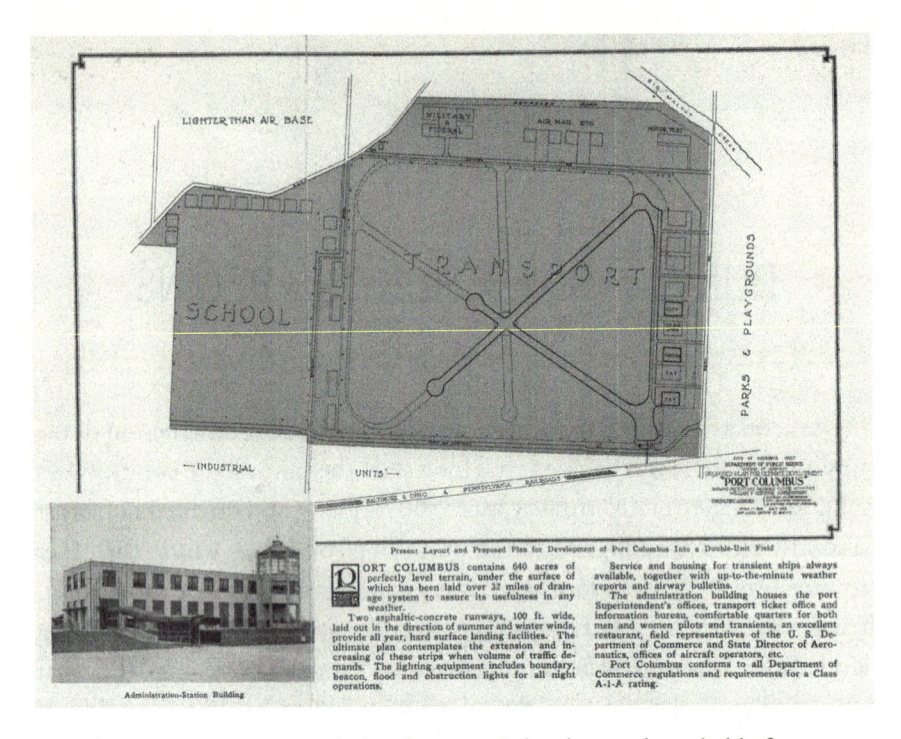

Photo showing proposed plan for Port Columbus with probable future activities. Notice "Buttons" on NE/SW and SE/NW runways.
Photo courtesy of Stork Collection: Stork _308

All of the runways and taxiways were concrete. "They are constructed of a 5-inch concrete base with a 1 ½ inch topping of asphaltic binder material, the surface of which is roughened to provide improved traction for tires."[242]

"...but smooth and even in contour, so that the water will flow across the surface to the drains along the sides. They have a slope of six inches in width...every one hundred feet."[243]

The Building of an Airport: Port Columbus

Photo of concrete machine laying down 5 inches of
concrete as it constructs the runways.
Photo courtesy of Stork Collection: Stork _106

Robert F. Kirk

Photo of concrete runway after being constructed to a thickness of 5 inches.
Photo courtesy of Stork Collection: Stork _107

The Building of an Airport: Port Columbus

Photo of asphalt machine laying down an inch of asphalt over
the concrete runways to aid in traction of landing aircraft.
Photo courtesy of Stork Collection: Stork _108

The space between the runways and the rest of the airport fields were sodded or seeded to make any landing area as smooth as a carpet.[244]

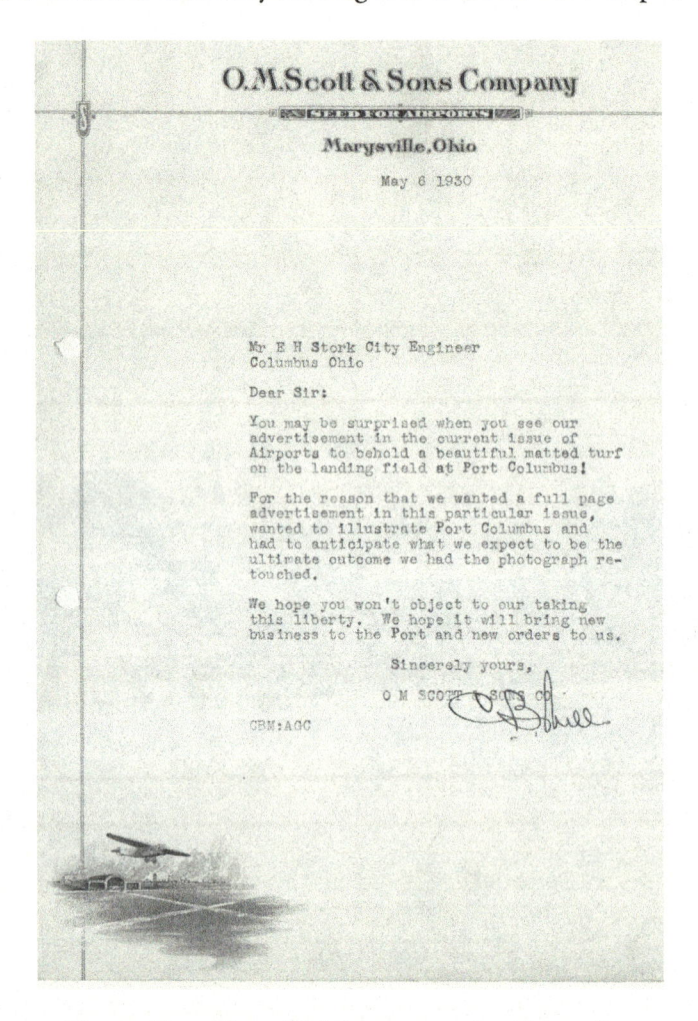

Photo of letter from OM Scott promoting the seeding
and sodding of the Port Columbus Airport field.
Photo courtesy of Ohio History Connection. #MSS454_B02_Mill_19300506.

It was even proposed that an underground tunnel be constructed leading from the Pennsylvania Railway Passenger Terminal under the Administration-Passenger Building to the awaiting Ford Tri-Motors in the departing area. These tunnels were discussed but they were never built. In place of the tunnel idea a long covered walkway was constructed that led

The Building of an Airport: Port Columbus

from the Pennsylvania Depot to the Administration/Passenger Building and then out to the waiting aircraft. This was a design that T.A.T. built into all of their passenger locations along the T.A.T. route.[245]

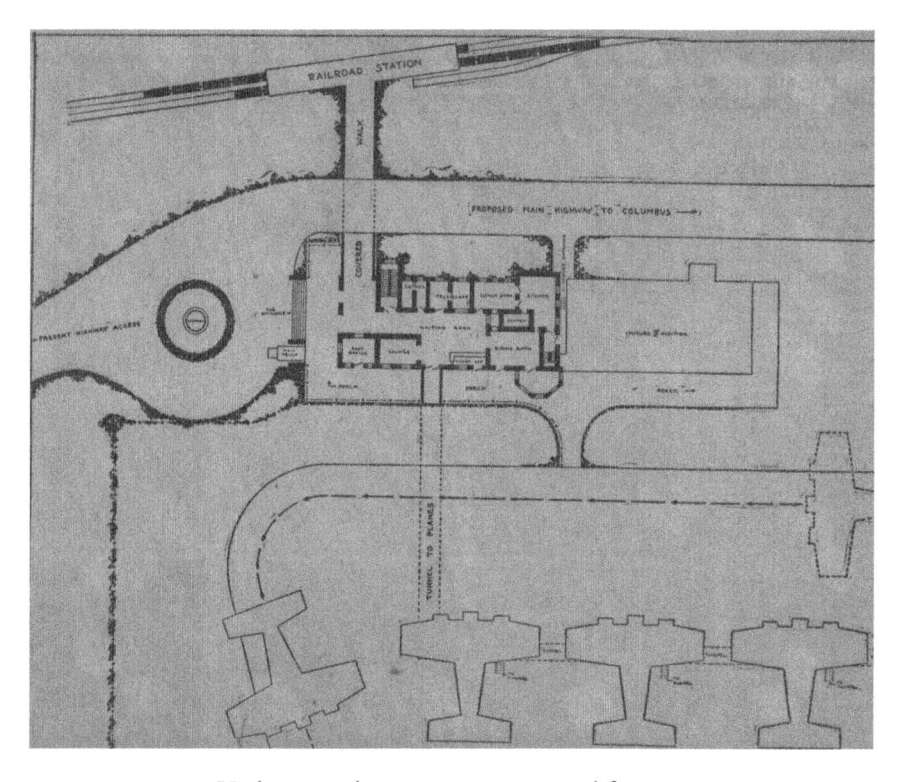

Underground passages are proposed for Port Columbus to move passengers to aircraft.
Photo courtesy of Stork Collection: Stork _289

"In the construction and planning of Port Columbus, no single feature has been overlooked and no expense has been spared to make it America's model airport."[246]

Based on his experience Stork knew the first task at hand was to clear the field of all brush and obstructions and then level the field. This airport plot was an excellent selection. With its only variance of 20 feet in elevation from the lowest portion of the field to the highest portion it was almost a perfectly level section of land. Of course it also had a fortunate drainage feature associated with the property with its two ditches that ran with a natural slope to Big Walnut Creek.[247] The drainage plan was to provide ample drain lines throughout the field that collected into trunk lines that then drained into the two ditches and emptied into the Big Walnut Creek.[248] This plan required hundreds of drainage lines filled with tiles that allowed the airport to drain all the water off the field in record time regardless of the amount of rain or snow that fell.[249]

AIRPORT LIGHTING AND AIRWAY SIGNS

With the lack of modern navigation aids it was helpful for cities and towns to put their names on the tops of barns and other easy to be seen landmarks. Larger cities with established airports erected multiple visual aids to help pilots identify the city by name. They put up arrows and signs giving directions to the airports.

"Thirty new airway markers will be erected within the vicinity of Columbus in the near future. The markers combine three points of guidance for passing pilots – wind direction, compass bearing and name of the community – and consists of a structural steel pole 25 feet in height, six inches in diameter. At the top of the pole is a windsock three feet in length, while eight feet below on a horizontal plane, is a large arrow 13 ½ feet long. This arrow, painted in chrome yellow will point toward the city and will bear the name Columbus in black. It is claimed the arrows are easily visible …at 3,000 feet minimum height and that the lettering designating the city is visible at 1000 feet."[250]

Landscape Air Marker
For parks, school yards, or along highways. Height of letters—20-foot minimum (50 feet preferable Color—shrubs with contrasting color flower border.

Highway Air Marker

Photo of aviation ground markings that show directional
and distance information to pilots in the air.
Airport Signs, Air Markings; Courtesy U.S. Department of Commerce,
Civil Aeronautics Administration, Bulletin No. 12. U.S. Government
Printing Office, Wash. D.C. Rev. 1949. Public Domain.

"The lighting system for the field is another large problem. According to the Department of Commerce regulations the boundary lights of the field must be marked by white lights, placed no closer than 250 feet apart. There are the beacons, landing lights, and signal lights required, besides lighting for buildings…This [lighting] project will probably do more for Columbus commercially, than any other single thing…"[251]

Airport leaders in the field knew airport lighting systems were soon to be required by the government. Modern airports needed to be open 24 hours a day and 7 days a week. For that to occur there had to be a night lighting system that assisted pilots to land their aircraft any time and in any weather. The Department of Commerce called this requirement A-1-A and Port Columbus wanted this rating.

The A-1-A Rating regulated by the Department of Commerce had many different requirements.

Department of Commerce Requirements:

1. At least one runway 2,500 feet in length with clear approaches
2. An airport beacon light
3. One or more hangars at least 80 by 100 feet sufficiently heated
4. Repair equipment sufficient to permit changing of engines and other major services
5. Weather instruments (With anemometer, barometer and thermometer)
6. Adequate snow removing equipment
7. Ambulance vehicle
8. Fire fighting equipment
9. Registration procedures for listing all planes arriving and departing
10. Sleeping quarters for at least three men
11. Waiting and rest rooms
12. Restaurant within one-half mile
13. Approved wind indicator
14. Fuel facilities
15. Communication and transportation facilities [252]

So Port Columbus was designed by Stork to meet all of the requirements of this rating. It included characteristics such as 24-hour service including boundary lights, flood and obstruction lights, runway lights and beacon code lights. These requirements were quite advanced for their time period.

Robert F. Kirk

Graphic design of Port Columbus showing airport lighting.
Photo courtesy of Stork Collection: Stork _246

Today, modern airports have much of the same lighting requirements.
There are still runway lights. They are a little different in that they come in three intensities. They can be adjusted for Low Intensity Runway Lights (LIRL), Medium Intensity Runway Lights (MIRL) or High Intensity Runway Lights (HIRL). These different lighting intensities can be adjusted by tower operators to accommodate changing weather conditions and for individual pilot preferences. If the tower is closed the lights can be controlled by the pilot in the air keying his mike on his radio a certain number of times. Seven times within 5 seconds will give HIRL, clicking the mike 5 times within 5 seconds will give MIRL and 3 times within 5 seconds will give the LIRL for the runway.

There are also runway end identifying lights (REIL), runway centerline lighting (CL) and touchdown zone lighting (TDZ).

For assistance in finding the runway during reduced visibility or low ceilings there are even lighting networks which are High Intensity Approach Lighting Systems with Sequenced Flashing lights (ALSAF). This lighting system is known as "The Rabbit." It is a series of bright lights that flash repeatedly from about a quarter of a mile out from the runway. It is very helpful in low ceilings or in reduced visibility conditions to help the pilot find the landing runway.

There are also Precision Approach Path Indicator Lights (PAPI) and Visual Approach Slope Indicator Lights (VASI) that assist pilots to fly the correct descent angle to the runway. This is helpful to pilots when it is very dark outside the cockpit or if the visibility is low with foggy or smoky conditions.

The early standards of airport lighting like those installed at Port Columbus are a great assist to night flying and aviation safety. These early beginnings showed how important airport lighting was and certainly found their way into modern airports.

A lot of research and planning enabled Port Columbus to meet the new Department of Commerce night lighting requirements.

Some of the lights required weren't even commercially available from reliable sources. To obtain the A-1-A rating on the air map of the nation, the airport had to provide 24-hour service and the field had to be equipped with boundary lights, beacon, flood and obstruction light illumination. In addition, on course and code lights (which flashed out "PC" for Port Columbus) were provided.[253]

Electrical work started with plans and specification. There were a great many things that didn't meet the needed requirement and the market didn't offer them, so Stork began the planning and designing of what was needed.[254]

Stork reported many days of anxiety in the testing of different apparatus to meet the needed requirements and the final selection of equipment meeting the specifications of the Department of Commerce. He also expressed how taxing it was letting contracts and proceeding along rapidly to complete the following:

1. The obstruction lights up
2. The boundaries marked
3. The beacon installed
4. The automatic control desk in operation
5. The lead in of 23,000 volts installed under the B&O Railroad tracks
6. Connection of electricity to the administration building.[255]

Boundary Lights

One of the first projects that Stork accomplished was that of boundary lights. Stork didn't like the types of boundary lights that were available. These standard lights were concreted into the ground. They were very stable, but that was the problem. If an aircraft ran into one of them it not only destroyed the boundary light but it did considerable damage to the aircraft. Stork didn't like this concept so he designed his own boundary light and tested it at Norton Field. "Following successful tests at Norton Field, a new type of boundary light, developed by Ernest H. Stork of the city engineering department will in all probability be specified for use on the new municipal airport. The light which is designed to collapse or tip over when struck by a plane…A number of accidents have occurred by ships striking immovable boundary lights and crashing. The chief advantage of the new light is that it can be struck by an airplane without damage to the ship and with but little damage to itself." [256]

The big advantage of the Stork Boundary Light was that it was not attached permanently to the concrete. There was a galvanized iron conical skirt that was supported by a conduit running through the skirt. The conduit was designed to break away from the concrete base without harming the aircraft or the boundary light. An electrical relay in the concrete base closed, and kept the electrical circuit connected to the other boundary lights, thus keeping them illuminated.

There would be little or no damage to the boundary light and it could be repaired or replaced within five minutes.[257]

The Building of an Airport: Port Columbus

Photo of boundary light designed by Stork.
Photo courtesy of Stork Collection: Stork _282

Photo of Stork's test of his boundary light.
Photo courtesy of Stork Collection: Stork _081

Photo showing Stork's boundary light breakaway design.
Photo courtesy of Stork Collection: Stork _359

Stork became famous for his development of the new boundary light system.

"Not only did he plan the port and its buildings but several of his inventions now are in use there. One of the most valuable is a movable boundary light, which was ridiculed as a 'dream' by engineers when Stork developed it, but is now in general use throughout the country and is manufactured by all leading companies specializing in airport materials."[258]

The type of light used in the boundary light was a General Electric, 60 C.P. 600 lumens light in clear glass, green and red. The light was designed to have a base 30 inches across and be 30 inches high. It was to be constructed of galvanized sheet metal and be painted chrome yellow.[259]

"The boundary light system consists of 52 lights spaced 300 feet apart and carried on low iron fixtures. A special fixture was developed by E. H. Stork, City Engineer of Columbus. It consists of a flat concrete marker or target through the center of which the lighting circuit cable comes up to a break-away pot. The conduit carrying the light rises from the cover of this pot."[260]

One estimate was that more boundary lights would be needed. This may have been because the field was planned to be increased in size in the near future. "For the boundaries, it is estimated that 90 white lights will be needed, while 30 red obstruction lights should be placed on various buildings… The field will be illuminated by six 3000-watt flood lights, while a 3,000,000 candlepower revolving beacon visible for many miles, will guide night flying pilots to Port Columbus."[261]

It was also decided that all of the wiring for the airport would be placed underground and a safe distance from the airport. This was to protect aircraft from obstructions when flying into Port Columbus. "All wires will be underground and for a short distance away for the port, they will also be carried underground, in order that a minimum of high obstructions will be in the way of ships coming in for a landing."[262]

Floodlights

General Electric Floodlights were the newest in the field and GE claimed it would furnish all the flood lighting necessary for Port Columbus.[263] Port Columbus became the first airport to adopt the floodlight system designed by the General Electric Company.[264]

All of the buildings at Port Columbus had floodlights illuminating them. "General Electric Flood lamp of 24 kilowatts rating, with eight 300-Watt lamps were selected for use at the 320-acre field. This would provide 2,000,000 total candlepower and an average illumination of .15 foot candles over the airport."[265]

Runway Lights

There were runway lights that lit both sides of each runway and showed their edges. This was very important to show the runway direction and layout for aircraft landing at night or in reduced visibility conditions.

There were almost 80 lights planned for installation on the 3500 and 2500-foot runways at Port Columbus.

The 77 lights placed 150 feet apart on both sides of the two runways indicated the hard surface channels and showed the exact elevation of the ground. The lights were set in concrete flush with the ground with the lenses designed to withstand great impact pressure. The runway lights were tested by Stork to make sure that they could withstand the impact of a transport plane landing on top of them. The tests revealed that one of the lens tested broke at 3,665 foot-pounds of pressure, and the other lens broke at 3,200 foot-pounds of pressure. The standard lens broke at 2,650 foot-pounds which was the equivalent of 30,000 pounds of weight. The newly selected Westinghouse lens broke at a pressure which was capable of withstanding an equivalent of 46,500 pounds. Thus the Westinghouse lens was considered as the best landing light lens for Port Columbus[266]

PROGRESS IN AIRPORT CONSTRUCTION

During May, the transport companies began to filter into the picture. This month T.A.T. began their excavations for their hangar. They built their radio station in March. The railroad began to construct the first train-plane depot in the country in May. Toward the end of May the administration building began showing above ground. By this date there were nine contractors all working hard to reach the goal of July 1, 1929 when the first T.A.T. services were to be inaugurated.[267]

Photo of Administration-Passenger Building showing above ground progress.
Photo courtesy of Stork Collection: Stork _165

Rotating Beacon

On top of the control tower of the administration building was a Crouse-Hinds revolving beacon of 6,000,000 candle power and two green on-course lamps flashing in Morse Code the letters "PC" meaning Port Columbus.

The beacon itself was very interesting. It had a one-piece convex lens of heat-resisting clear glass, directing 86% of the light in a concentrated upward beam at an angle of about 30 degrees. A magnetic lamp changer automatically triggered a spare lamp to come online if there was a failure of the first beacon. The beacon swept through an arch of 180 degrees. Its cycle was 10 seconds with the on-course lights flashing their signal for five seconds with an equal interval.[268]

This new type of revolving airport beacon had all of its moving parts enclosed in a glass dome. The pilots could see the beam from this very efficient system, on a clear night for 65 miles.[269]

Ceiling Lights

One very important feature of the new Port Columbus Airport was a device to measure the ceiling of the lowest cloud layer. This is very important information for pilots who are approaching to land at the airport. They may be flying above or in the clouds, and won't know what the cloud ceiling is above the ground. The pilots won't be able to descend safely through the clouds, see the airport and land visually on the runway.

Until relatively modern times, only a few major airports had this capability. Today with modern technology, special cameras and computer systems, hooked to an automatic broadcasting radio, airports can automatically transmit this information to pilots who are planning to land at the field. This is vital information for the safety of the flight.

This was an extremely advanced feature for an airport of this era. It certainly put Port Columbus Airport in a very competitive position compared to any other airport of its day.

The ceiling light that was installed at Port Columbus was a 500-watt, 14-inch ceiling light that was elevated to an angle of 63 degrees. The ceiling light was located on a steel tower 500 feet from the ceiling indicator, which was mounted on the roof of the administration building. It consisted of a metal arc graduated in feet, and a moveable sight with a pointer. Turning on the light, and leveling the sight on the spot where the beacon strikes the cloud layer, the height of the ceiling was obtained. The height of the spot (clouds) was read off directly in feet.[270]

Thus with this system airport officials could read the ceiling height at any time.

Obstruction Lights

Obstruction lights were used to illuminate all large buildings on the airport surface. It was a requirement in 1929 for all A-1-A airports certified by the Department of Commerce.

They were installed on the Port's hangars, administration building, and any other large structure located on the airport.

Approach Lights

At the ends of each of the runways were green approach lights. These lights showed the beginning and end of each of the runways designating where the pilots should position their aircraft to make a safe landing on the airport's runways.

Airport Weather

All of these required lighting additions to the Port Columbus Airport were vital to its operation 24 hours a day in all weather conditions. A study of the weather history of Port Columbus was accomplished to check and record what could be expected from the weather and what equipment was needed to meet the airport's demands.

The report showed:
Dense Fog Occurs:

1 Day per month in winter and infrequently during other seasons

Light Fog:

1 Day per month during spring and summer
2 Days per month during autumn and winter

Precipitation:

As heavy as 1 inch or more in 24 hours is recorded
1 Day in 2 months
Average monthly snowfall, Dec – March is about 6 inches
Nearest weather Bureau – Columbus, Ohio [271]

Wind-T

A Wind-T is a device that resembles an airplane and sits on the ground in a level position. It is free to rotate around in a 360 degree circle. It is aerodynamically designed to align itself into the prevailing wind. Usually there is a windsock that is attached on or near the Wind-T. The windsock is designed to lay flat if there is little or no wind. As the wind speed picks up and begins to blow harder the windsock rises up to a more upright position. As the wind blows harder the sock will continue to rise up until it is horizontal to the ground. This will indicate to the pilot that the wind is blowing at least 15 nautical miles per hour. The windsock will also align itself with the direction the wind. With the combination of both the Wind-T and the Windsock the pilot coming in for a landing can get a fairly good idea of the wind direction and speed.[272]

Photo of windsock at Port Columbus Airport.
Photo courtesy of Stork Collection: Stork _232

The meteorological conditions at the Port were considered good. The annual rainfall was about twenty-seven inches and not expected to ever interfere with flying. Snowfall averaged eight inches annually and was not expected to interfere with landings and take offs. But as a precaution the Port was being equipped with snowplows and a tractor to keep the runways clear.[273]

T.A.T. and Weather

Weather has always been recognized as the most hazardous component of flying. T.A.T. knew this and placed a high priority on weather forecast and reporting. They knew that the conditions of the weather couldn't be changed. The weather a pilot got was the weather he had to deal with.

However, areas or locations of adverse conditions could be recognized, along with their direction of movement and pilots could be warned to stay clear of these dangers.

To help with this issue, "Each field of the T.A.T. has it own experienced meteorologist, whose office adjoins the field manager's and which is in contact with radio stations by direct wire from each Port.

Any of these stations will answer the four fundamental questions the pilot wishes to know previous to take off, namely;

1. What weather conditions prevail at the destination?
2. What conditions will be encountered enroute?
3. What, when, and where changes may occur?
4. At what altitude will the most favorable flying conditions be found?"[274]

There were approximately 80 persons working all day long gathering data concerning the weather along the T.A.T.'s route. Ten are located at the main stops on the airway, with others working at intermediate towns and at a network of observation points situated both north and south of the route.[275]

The day for the meteorologists that staffed the T.A.T. stations was a long one. Their day normally began about 6:00 a.m. and continued until 7:00 or 8:00 p.m. The days had to be long because weather is a 24-hour a day event.

The weather reports that the meteorologists provided for the pilots had many different parts. The different parts of the measurements provided a weather puzzle to the airmen. It was with these different sections of the puzzle that the airmen could make good judgments concerning the weather expected at their destination. Thus the weather puzzle included wind speed and direction, visibility, sky condition, temperature, clouds, field observations and barometric pressure.[276]

All of the measured weather information was reported on a form and sent through the teletype machine to all of the T.A.T. stations along the route.

Telephone / Telegraph/Aircraft Radio

There was a telephone and telegraph facility at Port Columbus, and a radio station built by T.A.T. was only seven-tenths of a mile north of the field. The radio station operated twenty-four hours a day and was connected to the airport by a teletype system.[277] It was also connected to the T.A.T. Aircraft in the area.

Photo of radio used in the aircraft to talk to the T.A.T. Radio Station.
Photo courtesy of Stork Collection: Stork _263

Fire Protection & Fire Extinguishers

Fire protection was provided by an eight inch main which ran the length of the field behind the hangars. Future plans were to encircle the field and install a booster system to provide higher water pressure.

There were fire extinguishers placed in all the hangars on the field. Hand chemical extinguishers along with a light chemical truck were used to fight small fires.[278]

Airport Signs

There were several different types of airport signs placed at different locations at Port Columbus. They were thought to be important for safety of workers and passengers at the airport.

These signs included:

1. No Smoking in Hangars or Near Planes
2. Danger Low Flying Airplanes
3. Danger: Do not Touch Propellers
4. Free Parking
5. No Parking Please[279]

Aviation Map of the United States

There was an Aviation Map of the United States located in the Administration-Passenger Building. It was 6 feet tall and ten feet long. Pilots used this large map for flight planning. There were 100-mile circles placed on the map starting with Port Columbus at its center. Every 500 miles there was a heavy red circle.[280]

ACCIDENTS, LICENSING OF PILOTS, AIRPORT RULES

People at this time were very concerned about the safety of flight. There had been forty-seven deaths resulting from commercial aircraft operations in the United States in the first part of 1927. These results came from an aeronautical survey conducted by the Department of Commerce.[281]

The survey revealed some very interesting safety information. "The survey disclosed that practically all of the miscellaneous air accidents occurred with unlicensed pilots and unlicensed planes. The federal air laws required licensing of pilots and aircraft only in interstate flying."[282]

If a pilot was flying an unlicensed aircraft and he himself was unlicensed it wasn't against the law if he flew within his own state. Hard to believe today but that was the federal law back in 1927.

It was understood by those interested in the advancement of aviation in the United States that laws had to be changed so that all pilots and all aircraft were licensed if there was to be improvement in the aviation's safety records and make passengers feel safer about flying.

Port Columbus Superintendent William F. Centner developed a set of airport rules that was published and pilots were required to follow when taking off and landing at the field. There were also other rules that dealt with various safety and normal operating practices.

Robert F. Kirk

August 6, 1930.

Mr. H. S. Johnson, Pilot,
Continental Airways,
2420 South Parkway,
Chicago, Ill.

Mr. Johnson:-

I want to call your attention to two of the airport traffic rules which were violated by you this morning.

First: Ships with engines running are not to be abandoned by the pilot, unless another qualified pilot or a competent mechanic is placed in charge to attend the controls or, unless the switch is cut. I understand that you left your ship this morning long enough to run into the administration building for your clearance authority, leaving your ship unattended. While you may have been gone for only a few minutes, it is bad practice to abandon a ship on such circumstances and the regulations we have against it must be complied with.

The second matter I wish to call to your attention for correction was your trailing one of the T-A-T ships down the runway and then taking off ahead of it. This is wrong and dangerous. Hereafter under such circumstances please delay your start until any ships ahead of you have completed their take off, and keep in line. There probably was no imminent danger of collision on this mornings take off, but I think you can see for yourself the wisdom of each ship staying in its place and taking off in orderly fashion, where several departures are scheduled close together.

I hope you will understand this situation in the future and continue to give us your cooperation in carrying out operations satisfactorily, safely and for the best interests of all concerned.

Very cordially yours,

Wm. F. Centner,
Superintendent: PORT COLUMBUS.

WFC-L.

Photo of letter from Superintendent Centner correcting actions of a pilot who was operating his aircraft in an unsafe manner. Photo courtesy of the Ohio History Connection: #MSS454_B02_Centner_19300806

T.A.T.'S EARLY FORMATION

It is really hard to fully understand the impact Charles A. Lindbergh's flight across the Atlantic had on the development of all aspects of aviation in the United States and the rest of the world. In a day and a half he was able to demonstrate to the world what the future of aviation was going to look like.

"When Colonel Lindbergh made his flight across the Atlantic, all admired him...[it] stimulated an interest that will certainly bring about the advancement of aviation to a common commercial basis."[283] It began a realistic dream of what could take place in aerial transportation regarding the building of airplanes, airports and the movement of passengers.

"The air-mail line is no longer a dream. It is now one of our dependable common carriers...Manufacturers and distributors are buying planes to use for important business trips and rush deliveries. Airports are being established in our cities to accommodate commercial planes."[284]

One giant step in commercial passenger aviation came during a meeting after Lindbergh's flight.

A small group of men lingered over cigars and cigarettes in the dining room of the Engineer's Club in New York one evening in spring. It was shortly after Col. Charles A. Lindbergh's flight to Paris and the talk was of aviation, and the effect the flight would have upon commercial operations. "Think the transatlantic hop ever will become a commercial possibility?" questioned one of the men in the meeting. "No doubt of it at all," one replied. The discussion continued but took a fateful twist from that of transatlantic travel to that of transcontinental travel. "No use trying the Atlantic until we have our own country licked. What's the matter with a transcontinental line between here and Los Angeles? After we have that, let's try the Atlantic."[285]

The conversation then turned to what a route from New York to Los Angeles might look like. The men quickly found maps in the club's library and began to draw lines across the country in what might be possible routes. Many items were taken into consideration in drawing out the route across America. These men recognized the need to include the railroad in parts of the travel plans. Railroad timetables were consulted along with locations of train tracks and terminals close to possible cities that might become part of the route.

Some, but not all variables were anticipated, yet the initial transcontinental course that was penciled in that evening resembled a great deal of similarity to what eventually became the final one decided by these men. This fateful, informal meeting was the beginning of what became the Transcontinental Air Transport Company that established the first transcontinental airline passenger service in the United States.

"Colonel Lindbergh returned to the United States shortly after the discussion in the Engineer's Club took place. The plans were laid before him and he was asked for his opinion. The opinion was favorable and Colonel Lindbergh was asked to become a part of the organization with the office of Chairman of the Technical Committee."[286]

Lindbergh liked what he saw in the plans of the cross-country route and decided that he wanted to be part of the endeavor. He joined the company and was assigned the technical details of surveying the route structure and making recommendations on its final path. He was also responsible for all the aviation decisions of the plan including deciding on what aircraft was best suited for the passenger service.

The full company was formed shortly thereafter and included a number of prominent individuals that were involved in the aviation industry.

"Some of them were associated with Curtiss Aeroplane and Motor Company, others with National Air Transport and still others with Wright Aeronautical Corporation. There were also representatives of several banking firms including Blair and Company, New York; Knight, Dysart and Gamble, St Louis, and The State National Bank of St. Louis. The Pennsylvania Railroad Company, likewise was interested."[287]

Photo of Transcontinental Air Transport's original
Stock Certificate issued in 1928.
Photo courtesy of Liberty Aviation Museum, Port Clinton, Ohio.

With the formation of the new T.A.T. company the need was recognized to expand the Technical Committee headed by Lindbergh. There was a tremendous need for assistance provided to Lindbergh in the many travel plans and trips that were needed to gain information on the possible locations for the T.A.T. line. So others were added to help with the huge responsibilities. Lindbergh was to be the Chairman but with him were, "William B. Mayo, Chief Engineer for the Ford Motor Company, Charles S. 'Casey' Jones, President of Curtiss Flying Service, and Major Thomas Lanphier, until recently Commander of the First Pursuit Squadron of the Army Air Corps."[288]

Even though the initial T.A.T. route had been laid out by the men in the first meeting in New York City, there needed to be work accomplished on that route to make sure it was the best flight path across the country. One of the things that had to be considered was the weather patterns across the states. There were areas of increased moisture where the air is more humid and a major contributor to dangerous flying weather. When there is more moisture in the atmosphere it becomes less stable and more prone to phenomena such as thunderstorms, rain, hail, and freezing moisture that can cause aircraft icing. This is a very dangerous situation that can actually bring down an aircraft.

Just moving the proposed route a couple of hundred miles south along the track reduced the chances of these hazards.

The average temperature and dew point spread are also two major weather considerations. They can cause foggy conditions that can make pilots unable to find the runways.

Weather characteristics and patterns that had been documented historically were studied so that the best and safest route could be planned and selected.

The presence of existing railroad tracks and passenger depots along the possible routes were also studied and had a major impact on the final course.

High on the list of the items that were looked at for final selection of the T.A.T. route were the existence and location of airports across the states. Cities along the possible routes that already had transport capable airports, or cities able to expand into viable airports, became major players in the final course.

"In addition, T.A.T. wanted its fields located as near to the railroad lines as possible to facilitate the transfer of the passengers from the planes to trains, and vice versa. In fact it wanted its airport immediately adjacent to the railroads whenever such arrangements could be made. The airport problem was partially solved when four cities along the route agreed either to provide new airports or improve those already in existence. These cities were Columbus, St. Louis, Kansas City, and Wichita."[289] Indianapolis was another one of these possible locations except it was built by the state of Indiana and not by a local city.

Albuquerque, New Mexico and Los Angeles, California already had airports so T.A.T. leased land on these for use as landing locations. The Los Angeles location was at the Grand Central Air Terminal in Glendale, California. It was a well-established airport with modern concrete runways

The Building of an Airport: Port Columbus

and good weather conditions somewhat away from local foggy weather. It was also only about a 15-20 minute ride by car into city of Los Angeles.

The airport at Albuquerque needed some upgrading to meet the standards required by T.A.T. That was accomplished to make it a location selected by the company.

There were four more cities where the railroads were present but where no airports existed. These were Waynoka, Oklahoma; Clovis, New Mexico; Winslow, Arizona; and Kingman, Arizona. Land was either leased or purchased at all of these locations and airports were built there by T.A.T. All of these airports were out of the cities so they required some means of transporting passengers to the cities and train station locations.

To help in this transportation issue T.A.T. had a special trailer designed and built by the Curtiss Company. These were large modern comfortable trailers with usually 16 leather seats for passengers. T.A.T. purchased ten Studebaker Coupes with special hitches in the trunk area where the trailers could be attached. These special Curtiss trailers were called Aero Cars. They worked very well to move the passengers to and from the needed locations of airports, Harvey House restaurants, and train passenger terminals.

The locations of the new airports built by T.A.T. were only a few miles out of town. At Waynoka the T.A.T. Airport was about 5 miles north, northeast of town; at Clovis it was about 8 miles west of town; Winslow about three miles south of town and at Kingman approximately four miles north of town.

The airports at each of these four towns are now gone with one exception - Winslow, Arizona. The original T.A.T. terminal is still there, as well as the T.A.T. hangar. The Winslow Airport is in full operation there with the T.A.T. terminal in use as a Fixed Base Operation (FBO). The hangar is also in use. It is still only about 3-4 miles south of the city of Winslow.

It is certainly worth a stop there to see a special part of aviation history. The Winslow Airport is owned by the city of Winslow and operated as a municipal airport. A refurbished Fred Harvey Hotel and Restaurant is also there. It is named the La Posada. It is connected to the old Santa Fe Railroad Depot. The railroad yard nearby is fully operational.

The La Posada is located near the old Route 66 highway that runs through Winslow. Stopping off Interstate 40 onto the old Route 66 and finding the old Winslow Airport and Terminal/Hangar and the La Posada are certainly worth taking in as one of the historical landmarks of aviation.[290]

On the original route that was outlined in New York City, the T.A.T. route was to go though Dodge City, Kansas and Las Vegas, New Mexico. The final route was changed and did not use these two locations. The final T.A.T. route was New York City to Port Columbus, Ohio by Pennsylvania Railroad by night. Then flight on Ford Tri-Motors to Stout Field (Indianapolis); St. Louis, Missouri (Lambert Field), Kansas City Municipal Airport; Kansas City, Missouri; Wichita Municipal Airport, Kansas; Waynoka Airport, Oklahoma; Clovis (Port Air), New Mexico; Albuquerque Airport, New Mexico; Winslow Airport, Arizona ; Kingman Airport, Arizona; Grand Central Air Terminal, Glendale, California. "[291]

Lindbergh announced that service of the Transcontinental Air Transport Company was to be divided into eastern and western divisions.[292] The eastern division went from New York to Waynoka, Oklahoma. The western division went from Los Angeles, California to Clovis, New Mexico. The Santa Fe Railroad connected the two divisions and ran between Waynoka, Oklahoma and Clovis, New Mexico.

Lindbergh also announced that he was making inspections of all of the terminals along the route before it opened. He actually flew the route several times across the U.S. to make sure that the selection of the route was the best possible. He flew his Ryan Brougham across the U.S. as he worked out the new line. It was a fast aircraft and allowed him to quickly move across the country. Franklin Mahoney, the owner of the Ryan Aircraft Company gave the Brougham plane to Lindbergh. The Brougham was given as a replacement aircraft because Lindbergh had donated the Spirit of St. Louis to the Smithsonian Museum.

He also flew the route at the Ford Tri-Motor airspeed to check for timing for the final published flight timetable. Lindbergh used a Curtiss-Falcon aircraft to check on the accuracy of the timetable. It was a slower aircraft that flew about the same speed as the larger Ford Tri-Motor. He made sure that what had been planned for so many months would be ready to go and that the timetables that were published would be accurate and grounded in reality.

The Building of an Airport: Port Columbus

It is worth noting that the railroads' involvement in the establishment and operation of T.A.T. were in the planning from the beginning. It had to be, if the timeline for the required reduced time across the country was possible. T.A.T. advertised that the trip by plane and train would cut the travel time in half. It reduced the time required to travel by rail, which was four days or 96 hours, down to 48 hours.

At the time commercial passenger travel by air at night was not authorized. First there weren't airports with adequate airport lighting for night flying and second there were no reliable navigation systems in existence for night flying. So, T.A.T. had to use the trains for night movement of passengers to save the time needed to realize the goal of a 48 hour cross country trip.

Lindbergh did foresee a time when aircraft would fly at night and that passengers would be part of that experience. However, it was understood by the founders of T.A.T. that there would always be a place in the movement of cargo and passengers on the railroad system. They saw both plane and train travel as vital components of the future where one mode of travel would compliment the other.

PORT COLUMBUS INAUGURATION: OPENING AN AIRPORT

For over a year aviation authorities in America had been carefully building the needed ground facilities for T.A.T. as it reached from New York to Los Angeles. Every contingency had been foreseen and met with the latest equipment produced by science.[293] In fact 5 million dollars was placed on account to build the facilities, purchase the equipment and hire the needed men and women to make the T.A.T. a success. This was to ensure that the passengers on the new airline service had the most dependable, comfortable, speedy and safe air transportation possible.[294]

Henry Ford, was one of the dignitaries present at the opening of Port Columbus. He was a major contributor to the success of the adventure, building the Ford Tri-Motor airplane, which was the main aircraft used in beginning the T.A.T. line. He said, "The inauguration of the service [T.A.T.] is the most important event since the spanning of the continent by the railroads."[295] Ford made several supportive remarks concerning this important inaugural event but one such comment was particularly important concerning aviation. "When a company at once so conservative and progressive as the Pennsylvania adopts aviation as auxiliary, it indicates the final official approval of the modern airplane as a common carrier and as an integral part of our system of communications. The alliance of air and rail, completed at Columbus today, is an event of historical importance."[296]

Many speeches were given over the three-day inauguration event in Columbus. Some were short and to the point while others were longer and sometimes nondescript.

Yet, T.B. Clement, who was the General Traffic Manager for T.A.T., gave a summary of the accomplishments of T.A.T. and the railroads in the establishment of the 48-hour trip from the east coast to the west coast in both a philosophical and poetic statement.

Spanning the American continent has developed within its comparatively short history, into a process of moving its coast lines nearer to each other. The moving process started at scratch with the coast months apart. The railroad and the motorcar reduced the distance to terms of weeks and finally of days. Now comes the airplane and terms adopted for distance become 'hours.' Perhaps that changing of terms – from months, to weeks, to days and finally to hours is the most romantic phase of an essentially romantic undertaking. The term miles loses its significance as a measure of long distance and transportation becomes a problem not of defeating distance, but in defeating time – a race against the hour hand on a clock rather than a marathon with a calendar.[297]

The official opening of Port Columbus to the public was Monday, July 8, 1929. However, there was a three-day period from Saturday, July 6 through Monday, July 8 for all kinds of programs, speeches and displays that were open to the public. They were days filled with a long list of activities. In fact dedication for the event was a full three-day celebration that filled the morning, afternoon and evening hours. This Dedication Program lists the many events.

PROGRAM

SATURDAY, JULY 6

3:00 to 3:45 p.m.—Exhibition flying by Red Jackson, Curtiss Flying Service; John Stewart, Monosport plane, and Fred Lund, Waco Mfg. Co., Troy, Ohio.
4:00 p.m.—Parachute jumping by army pilots.
4:30 p.m.—Passenger flying.
10:00 p.m.—Pyrotechnical display, Welsch Aircraft Mfg. Co., Anderson, Ind.

SUNDAY, JULY 7

1:00 to 3:00 p.m.—Passenger flying.
3:00 p.m.—Exhibition flying by Red Jackson and Fred Lund.
4:00 p.m.—(1) Parachute jumping for accuracy.
(2) Landing to mark.
(3) Bombing for accuracy.
5:00 to 6:00 p.m.—Passenger flying.
Band Concert during entire afternoon by American Legion Band.

MONDAY, JULY 8

7:35 to 8:15 a.m.—Arrival of "Airway Limited" over the Pennsylvania Railroad, transfer of passengers to TAT plane, take-off of first transcontinental plane.

10:00 a.m.—Dedication ceremonies. Addresses will be made by Governor Myers Y. Cooper of Ohio; Mayor James J. Thomas of Columbus; representatives of Transcontinental Air Transport, Inc. and the Pennsylvania Railroad Co., and Government officials.

Passenger flying balance of day.

Special privileges for visiting guests will be arranged.

Photo of Port Columbus Dedication Days Schedule.
Photo courtesy of Stork Collection: Stork _162

Parking facilities for approximately 25,000 automobiles each day of the three day period had been provided on the airport and adjacent to Port Columbus.[298]

Photo of congested parking on Inauguration Day, July 8, 1929.
Photo courtesy of Chuck Blardone Collection.

T.A.T. was ready for the inaugural event to take place, however every part of the new Port Columbus Airport wasn't ready. The two runways were ready for takeoffs and landings but the runways weren't finished in length. The southwest end of the long runway wasn't completed nor was the northwest end of the shorter southeast to northwest runway.

The Administration-Passenger Building wasn't finished but was open for inspection. The covered walkways that ran from the railroad depot up to the Administration-Passenger Building, and from there to the flight line, where the aircraft were waiting were all completed.

The T.A.T. Hangar was also completed and ready for operation. The new Curtiss Hangar and the Municipal Hangar had been started but construction wasn't complete.[299]

On Saturday there were parachute jumps, passenger flights during the day and pyrotechnical displays at night. On Sunday there were parachute jumps, passenger flights, exhibition flights and a band concert in the afternoon.

Monday was the long awaited Inauguration Day! The day when the opening and dedication of Port Columbus Airport took place. It was also the first day of the opening of the new T.A.T. transcontinental airline passenger service across the United States.

The day began at 7:55 a.m. with the arrival of the "Airway Limited," the name given to the special Pennsylvania Railroad train that began in New York City, the night before, carrying the first T.A.T. passengers to Port Columbus.

Amelia Earhart was one of the "Airway Limited" passengers coming in from New York. Miss Earhart gained fame when she became the first woman to make the flight across the Atlantic. She was a passenger during the flight and not the pilot of the aircraft. However, she was a pilot with approximately 500 hours in the air.[300] A shortage of fuel prevented her and the aircraft crew from making their destination without refueling.

She was employed by T.A.T. to write columns in PlaneTalk, T.A.T.'s publication, as well as other magazines and newspapers of the time concerning how women could be involved in aviation. She encouraged flying for women not only as passengers but also on becoming pilots themselves and flying their own planes. She wrote about proper dress for women as they became involved in flying.

The passengers were quickly moved from the train platform to the airport station office. During the 50-60 yards travel distance, they were greeted by T.A.T. officials.

Robert F. Kirk

Current photo showing the distance that was needed to travel from the train platform to the T.A.T. Passenger Building. Photo by author.

There was no time to lose, as the big Ford Tri-Motors were scheduled to depart at 8:15 a.m. The passenger bags were taken to the awaiting aircraft where they were quickly loaded in the wing cargo areas. There was only time for a few greetings with dignitaries and a quick comfort break. Then off they went through the double doors on the north side of the Administration-Passenger Building, along the covered walkway and boarded onto the shiny new large Ford Tri-Motors. There were ten such aircraft that were part of the fleet of Tri-Motors. The two Ford Tri-Motors that were there that first morning, representing T.A.T.'s commercial fleet, were the City of Columbus and the City of Wichita.

The Building of an Airport: Port Columbus

Photo of passengers being loaded onto Ford Tri-Motor
while their bags are loaded into its wings.
Photo courtesy of Chuck Blardone Collection.

There were scores of dignitaries present for this historic aviation event. "Between 5,000 and 6,000 people braved a drizzle to witness the transfer of passengers from trains to planes and dedication of Port Columbus, the new municipal airport."[301]

"In Washington, Secretary of Commerce Lamont pressed a button in his office, a gong sounded at the airport here, an official waved his hands and the City of Columbus took off for Indianapolis."[302] The City of Wichita followed a few minutes later.

Photo of the City of Columbus and City of Wichita getting ready for takeoff at Port Columbus on July 8, 1929. Photo courtesy of Stork Collection: Stork _083

Photo of the City of Columbus and City of Wichita just before takeoff at Port Columbus on July 8, 1929. Photo courtesy of Columbus Regional Airport Authority.

It wasn't really a good day for flying. It was a rainy day with cloudy skies. Yet it was a great day for aviation and the brand new airline passenger service.

As both aircraft climbed through the cloudy skies they received a weather report from the nearby weather station. The aircraft were relayed some valuable information.

The weather station had detected an area of bad weather along the two aircrafts' planned flight paths. The planes were advised to deviate from their proper course to divert around the storm threat. The two Tri-Motors modified their direction of flight and missed the growing threat. The two aircraft quickly diverted around the storm and flew clear of both bad weather and clouds. Clear of the storms now and flying in favorable conditions the two aircraft resumed their course to Indianapolis.[303] Each ship was carrying 10 passengers.[304]

This marvel of safety, on relaying almost real time weather from the ground weather station to each individual aircraft, was a first for an aviation company. First, it required a first class functioning national system of weather stations that could collect vital weather data and then send it along to other ground stations and inflight aircraft. This required an elaborate system of ground teletype machines all connected to send the weather data along to other stations.

Second, the ground stations and each aircraft needed powerful radio transmitters and receivers that could send and receive the weather information. T.A.T. spared no expense in developing such weather recording and transmitting capabilities.

Their radios also had another built in feature that provided enhanced safety to each aircraft with their radios installed. It provided the ground station the ability to locate an aircraft that might have become lost in bad weather, or one unable to locate the landing field because of low visibility or ceilings. It worked by the ground radio station receiving a long auditory signal from the lost aircraft. By means of triangulation, the ground station could locate the position of the aircraft. "The radio communication consists of two elements…first the radio direction installation and second radio communication both ways. The directional radio has been worked out in close cooperation between the government and the radio companies, and this installation which will give the pilot his general location at all times while in the air, both day and night..."[305]

C. M. Keys, President of Transcontinental Air Transport, Inc. talked about how vast and important this system of aerial communication was for safety of flight for T.A.T.'s fleet of aircraft.

"Direct communication at all times between airplane and the ground, between ground points, airports, air fields, and back again to planes in the air, the whole system extending for more than 2000 miles [will] soon to be incorporated as one great air travel safety factor in the Lindbergh Line."[306]

Meanwhile, at Port Columbus the dedication programs continued. At 8:30 a.m. a large pancake breakfast began in the T.A.T. hangar. The dignitaries filled the hangar space designated for the breakfast. T. B. Clement, General Traffic Manager for T.A.T. was in charge of the event. Notables scheduled at the breakfast included Henry Ford, his son Edsel Ford, Harvey Firestone, the founder of the Firestone Tire and Rubber Company, and W. W. Atterbury, President of Pennsylvania Railroad. Atterbury wasn't able to attend but was represented by Elisha Lee, Executive Vice President of the Pennsylvania Railroad.[307]

Transcontinental Air Transport, Inc.
Mr. T. B. Clement, General Traffic Manager
has the honor
of requesting your presence at
Breakfast
eight-thirty o'clock, Monday, July 8, 1929
in the TAT Hangar
Port Columbus

Immediately following the ceremonies incident to the inauguration of Coast-to-Coast Air-Rail passenger service and the dedication of Port Columbus - the Eastern Air Terminal of TAT

Please send acceptance by return mail,
or not later than June 29, care
Mr. Kline L. Roberts
66 East Broad St., Columbus, Ohio

Photo of T.A.T. invitation for breakfast to dignitaries.
Photo courtesy of Stork Collection: Stork _044

Robert F. Kirk

NOTABLES GATHER AT AIRPORT DEDICATION. *Left to right in center:* Elisha Lee, vice president of Pennsylvania Railroad; Henry Ford, Harvey S. Firestone and Edsel Ford, are shown during exercises at Port Columbus opening. —Sunday Journal Photo.

Photo of Elisha Lee, Pennsylvania Railroad; Henry Ford,
Harvey S. Firestone and Edsel Ford shown during activities
at Port Columbus Inauguration on July 8, 1929.
Photo courtesy of Stork Collection: Stork _124

The Building of an Airport: Port Columbus

Henry and Edsel Ford left Detroit, Sunday midnight, on a special train of three cars. They arrived in Columbus at 5:30 a.m. Monday. The special train waited for the Fords and returned them to Detroit after the dedication program.

William P. Mayo, Vice President of the Ford Company, and head of the Stout Aircraft Company, which built the large Ford Tri-Motor aircraft for T.A.T., was also present and accompanied the Ford group to the ceremonies.[308]

The Saturday night light exhibit was one talked about for weeks. It involved turning on the mass of lights available at Port Columbus for all to see.

"The Port, Saturday night shone like a jewel on the eastern rim of the city. All lights including boundary lights, ceiling lights, hangar floodlights, the 3,000,000 candle-power beacon light with its 'PC' code on-course light and the 8,000,000 candle power flood light, were turned on for the first time."[309]

Also present were Myers Cooper, Ohio Governor; David S. Ingalls, Assistant Secretary of the Navy in Charge of Aeronautics; Director of Public Service, W. H. Duffy; General Dennis E. Nolan and John M. Vorys, State Director of Aeronautics.[310]

On the west coast the operation of T.A.T. was also swinging into operation. The night before, "Charles A. Lindbergh touched an electric button in Los Angeles...officially opening the train-plane service of the Transcontinental Air Transport, the Pennsylvania and the Santa Fe railways. As Col. Lindbergh pressed the electric button a signal was flashed to New York and the Airway Limited of the Pennsylvania Railroad left its terminal there with 16 passengers of the train-plane service...whose rail trip last night carried them to Columbus, Ohio. Colonel Lindbergh will fly the east bound plane to Winslow only, where the regular pilot will bring the ship to Clovis."[311]

Colonel Lindbergh did fly the City of Los Angeles to Winslow where he and his bride spent the night. Another crew took the City of Los Angeles on to Clovis.

The next afternoon Lindbergh was to fly the City of Los Angeles back west. However it was damaged on takeoff at Clovis. The pilot of the craft was J.B. Stowe. He took a reserve aircraft, the City of San Francisco, and flew it to Winslow to deliver Lindbergh's westbound passengers. Stowe was late arriving in Winslow. As soon as Stowe landed Lindy took the controls of the City of Philadelphia and took off for Los Angeles. On board were his wife Anne, Amelia Earhart and other westbound dignitaries from the east. The second aircraft bound for Los Angeles with the other westbound passengers was the City of Washington. It had to hold over Los Angeles so Lindbergh could land first. Lindbergh had to make up lost time because of the City of Los Angeles incident.[312]

The dream for the establishment of a major modern airport in Columbus was realized with the first flight through Columbus by the newly established T.A.T. Transcontinental Airline Passenger service. It began its flying schedule in Port Columbus and continued its westward path across the continent to the western end of the line at Grand Central Air Terminal in Glendale, California. The reality of a great "Air Harbor" in Columbus and a successful transcontinental passenger service by T.A.T. were both major highlights in the development of aviation in America.

WOMEN'S AIR DERBY – AUGUST 1929: PORT COLUMBUS PROMOTES WOMEN'S AVIATION

Another significant event in the history of Port Columbus was the Women's Air Derby in August 1929. This was the first of its kind in aviation history. It began in Santa Monica, California and was a planned 8-day race that ended in Cleveland, Ohio after a last night rest and celebration in Port Columbus. The race began with 20 women entered, 18 of which were from the United States.

Fourteen pilots were in the heavy plane category and six were in the lighter aircraft class.

<u>Some well known names in aviation that flew in the race included:</u>

1. Florence "Pancho" Barnes
2. Marvel Crosson
3. Ruth Elder
4. Louise McPetridge Thaden
5. Ruth Nichols
6. Amelia Earhart[313]

Amelia took third place in the First Women's Air Derby.
Photo of Amelia Earhart dressed in flight jacket, helmet
and goggles. Handwritten note at lower right corner reads:
Amelia Earhart. Given by her Mother, 1940.
Photo courtesy National Air and Space Museum,
Smithsonian Institution, NASM 78-16945.

It was an exciting time for the start of the race that began at 2 p.m. The flyers would depart at one to two-minute intervals. There were over 3,000 spectators present for the start of the race. The prize money for the pilots in the race was $25,000.[314]

The first leg of the race was from Santa Monica to San Bernardino, California. This was only a 60-mile leg and took about 30 minutes to complete. In fact the leader in the first leg came in at a time of 32 minutes and 15 seconds.

This first leg was short but it gave the women pilots time to check out their aircraft and make sure everything was in order for the trip which was approximately 2,800 miles long. It also gave time for reporters and others interested in the contest to see the aircraft and talk to the pilots. Will Rogers was present at this landing point and he observed the lady pilots fixing their makeup after landing. He remarked, "This looks like a powder puff derby to me."[315] The name stuck and has been used in referring to this historic race ever since.

The 2,800 miles was a very long distance to travel considering the lack of navigation aids that were available at the time. Also it was long considering the fragile construction of aircraft of the day and even the aviation requirements for the pilots entered in the race. Each pilot was only required to have a total of 100 hours of flight time, with 25 hours of cross-country time in order to enter the race. This wasn't a lot of flight experience considering the type of aircraft that they flew and the large distances that they would have to travel. However, it was the same hour requirement of that imposed on the men pilots in the National Air Derby planned in Cleveland the next week.

The women pilots spent the night in San Bernardino and got ready for the next leg of the flight the following morning. The next leg of the race was to be from San Bernardino to Yuma, Arizona and then on to Phoenix for a 2nd night layover.[316]

Tragically, this next leg of the race involved half a dozen mishaps including one fatality. Marvel Crosson was found dead in the wreckage of her aircraft in what was believed to be an attempted forced landing.

"She met death in a forced landing. The left wing of her plane, in which she was enroute to Phoenix from Yuma yesterday in the National Air Derby was crumpled from hitting a bank."[317] It is believed that during her emergency landing in the desert she was thrown from her aircraft and killed. She was wearing a parachute but it was only partially opened.

After an investigation it was believed she suffered carbon monoxide poisoning from exhaust from her engine. It was speculated that she was rendered unconscious or incapacitated from the fumes.

This became a recognized problem for seven of the Beech aircraft used in the air race. Beech Travel Airs were made by the Beech aircraft company. Louise Thaden became ill while flying her Travel Air to Santa Monica before the race started. After landing, and climbing out of the cockpit, she fell ill to the ground.

After investigation it was discovered that exhaust fumes were coming into the cockpit. Beech's solution was to mount a four-inch hose from the leading edge of the engine cowling into the cockpit to bring fresh air to the pilot. This solved the problem as long as the pilot kept her nose in the hose breathing fresh oxygen.

Photo of Louise Thaden who became the winner of the first annual Women's Air Derby in 1929 flying through Port Columbus. She also won the Bendix Transcontinental Air Race the first year women were allow to race against men. She was one of the founding members of the Ninety-Nines, was named female aviator of the year and won many other awards during her flying career. She was the first woman pilot to achieve a pilot's license in the state of Ohio. She was also an author writing *High Wide and Frightened* and many aviation articles.
Photo courtesy National Air and Space Museum, Smithsonian Institution, NASM 83-2132.

The Building of an Airport: Port Columbus

Three other women pilots made forced landings during this leg of the race but all of them escaped injury.

Sabotage was hinted because so many of the lady pilots were having trouble with their aircraft. Claire Fahy had been forced out of the race at Calexico, California when support wires of her plane had been severed. Thea Rasche had to stay the night at Phoenix after foreign matter was found in her gasoline tank, resulting in a loss of engine power and a landing that damaged her plane's undercarriage.[318] Ruth Elder reported oil and gasoline had been intermixed in servicing her plane in San Bernardino.

These events, along with the death of Miss Crosson, prompted the San Bernardino District Attorney to investigate the handling of the planes at the San Bernardino Airport. The results of the investigation didn't find any evidence of sabotage.[319]

The route taken by the pilots for the 1929 Air Race included: Santa Monica to San Bernardino, California, to Phoenix (with an optional stop at Yuma, AZ), to El Paso, Pecos, Midland, Abilene, and Fort Worth, Texas, to Wichita, Kansas City, Kansas, East St. Louis, Illinois, Terra Haute, Indiana, Cincinnati, Port Columbus and then finish at Cleveland, Ohio.

At Yuma, Amelia Earhart's airplane nosed over while she was getting ready to take off and broke the propeller. She had it replaced and continued the race.

A sand storm stopped the race in El Paso for the night. On the next leg of the race Blanche Noyes detected an in-flight fire in her baggage area. She made an emergency landing and put out the fire that seemed to be caused by a burning cigarette that had been thrown into her aircraft. She didn't smoke.

Pancho Barnes had even more serious trouble as she was landing at the Pecos field. A car got through the barriers by the runway and turned in front of Barnes as she was landing. Because the nose of her aircraft was so high for landing she couldn't see the car. She hit it and her aircraft was totaled. She wasn't hurt but couldn't continue the race because of damage to her aircraft.[320] She proceeded to Wichita in a relief aircraft and her plane was dismantled and shipped back to the factory for repair.[321]

While landing at Wichita, Kansas the lady pilots saw a crowd of spectators numbering over 10,000 people.

From Wichita the flyers traveled to Kansas City and then to East St. Louis. There were still 15 pilots in the race with Louise Thaden leading all the entrants.[322]

"Sunday morning the women flyers will leave East St. Louis at 9 a.m. They will stop at Terra Haute and Cincinnati leaving the latter city for Columbus at 4:30 p.m. They will take off at 12:30 p.m. Monday for Cleveland."[323]

There had been a number of incidents that hindered the lady pilots. These included May Halzlip experiencing a broken gasoline line; Blanche Noyes…smashing the landing gear of her plane and pancaking onto a landing field; Neva Paris damaging her plane when she overshot the runway and ran onto a roadway and nosed over; and Bobbie Trout badly damaging her plane during a forced landing.[324]

Louise Thaden was leading the race when the group of lady flyers landed at Port Columbus. They were to stay the night and celebrate their accomplishment at the Deshler-Wallick Hotel with an Aeronautical Banquet. They then took off the next day for a short flight to Cleveland for the finish of the race.

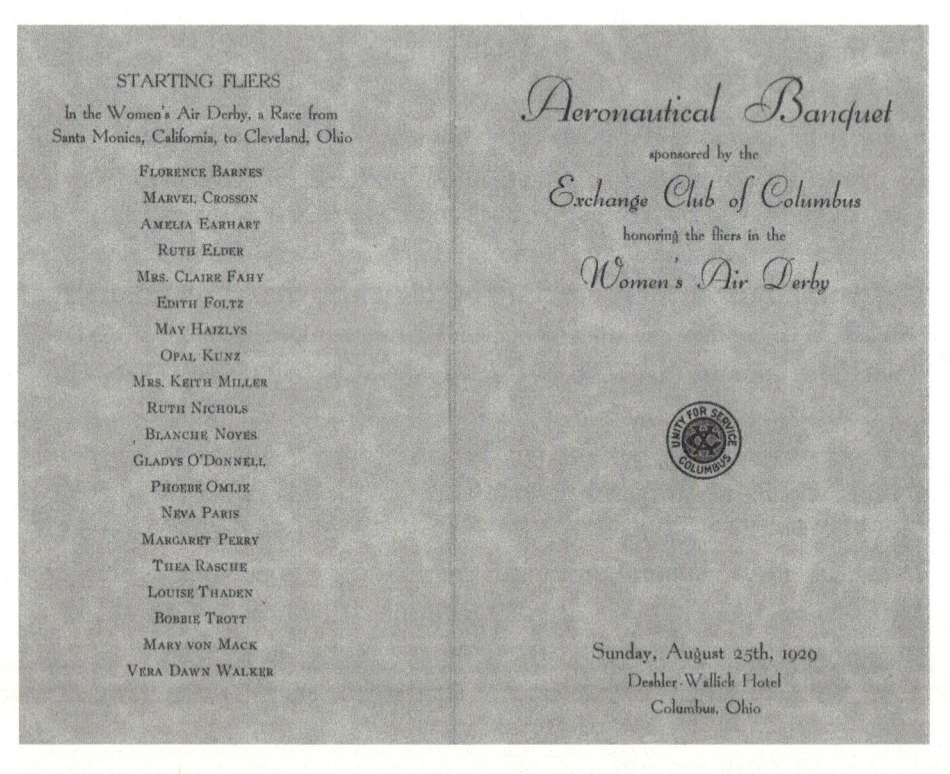

Photo of Aeronautical Banquet brochure honoring the fliers in the Women's Air Derby in Columbus, Ohio.
Photo courtesy of Stork Collection: Stork _223

Ruth Nichols was in third place in the race on Monday morning as the pilots prepared for one last short leg to Cleveland. Ruth Nichols wanted to do a test flight before the last leg began. It didn't turn out so well for her.

The new concrete runway at Port Columbus wasn't completed and was still under construction. The first portion of the concrete runway was closed. A large steamroller was working at the edge of the runway where the usable portion began. As Ruth attempted to take off she drifted into the steamroller and flipped upside down into a pile of loose dirt. She wasn't hurt as her safety belt held her securely. She was helped out of the aircraft but her hopes for completing the race were over.[325]

Ruth Nichols flew a Lockheed Vega. It was with this aircraft that in 1931-32 she became the only women to hold at one time the women's world speed, altitude, and distance records. Photo courtesy National Air and Space Museum, Smithsonian Institution, NASM 79-3164.

"Ruth Nichols...lost her place as third in the women's air derby, Monday afternoon, when her plane was wrecked as it struck a tractor at Port Columbus, while she was preparing to take off for Cleveland, on the final leg of the race across the country."[326]

"Ladybirds fly away home –which they did from Port Columbus at 1:35 p.m. Monday. Their home was the finish goal line at the Cleveland airport… from Santa Monica, Calif. in the first Women's air derby."[327] There was an estimated crowd of 20,000 people attending the end of the women's first air derby.

Louise Thaden won first place in the heavy aircraft category with a time of 20 hours, 19 minutes and 4 seconds. The next finishers were Gladys O'Donnel, Amelia Earhart, Blanche Noyes and Ruth Elder. Phoebe Omlie took first place in the lighter aircraft category with a time of 25 hours, 12 minutes and 47.5 seconds.[328]

In 1936 Louise Thaden and Blanche Noyes would go on to win the Bendix Trophy of the National Air Race when men and women were allowed to compete together for the first time.[329]

The Building of an Airport: Port Columbus

Blanche Noyes placed fourth in the first Women's Air Derby. She was the copilot for Louise Thaden when Thaden won the 1936 Bendix Trophy Race first time racing against men. For many years, she was the only woman pilot allowed to fly a government aircraft. She was the author of many newspaper and aviation magazine articles. She was inducted into the Aviation Hall of Fame in 1970. Photo courtesy National Air and Space Museum, Smithsonian Institution, NASM 97-15069.

SELECTED OHIO AVIATION "GIANTS"

Foster A. Lane

Foster A. Lane earned distinction in the history of Ohio aviation through his vast experiences in the field. He was born in 1903, the year of the first Wright flight and became interested in aviation at a very early age.

He purchased his first airplane in 1928 when he was just 25 years of age. During his many years of flying he was involved in varied aspects of aviation.

These included flying as:

1. Barnstormer
2. Aerobatics pilot
3. Flight instructor
4. Charter pilot
5. Test pilot
6. Aircraft exporter worldwide.

Photo of Foster Lane standing in front of Lane Aviation and his aircraft. (c.1955) Photo courtesy of Columbus Dispatch.

He was also an aviation author who wrote about his life in aviation in his work, *Log Book,* that was published in 1977. In this excellent work he described so much of his history in aviation and the exciting experiences he had during those years. He told of the engine failures and emergency landings that he lived through. He talked about the loss of friends that were not as fortunate as they died at an early age in their pursuit of flight. He described how hard it was to make a living in aviation and the many ups and downs encountered by a young person trying to be successful in the field. Making a go of it in aviation seemed to always go from boom to bust. He remarked, with a sense of humor, that of all the dangers in aviation, the greatest danger was "starving to death."[330]

In *Log Book* he gave a fantastic look at the history and development of many models of aircraft describing their designers' ideas and trials, along with their successes and failures moving aircraft development forward.

He knew and worked with such giants in the field of aviation as Walter Beech, Clyde Cessna, Lloyd Stearman and Al Mooney along with many others.

He participated in his younger years in the development of several aviation companies and observed as they prospered and then failed as the economic conditions of the country changed. He participated in the various struggles that occurred during the Great Depression of 1929. Through it all he learned what worked and what didn't work in the business of aviation. With this knowledge and limited funding he, along with his wife Ruth, worked to establish their own aviation business or Flight Base Operation (FBO) as they began to be called.

He established his FBO at Port Columbus in Hangar One. This was the old T.A.T. hangar that was built by the company in 1929. There he continued his FBO and aircraft sales business for several years.

He shared Hangar One with Knight K. Culver who designed and built aircraft. One of these aircraft was the Dart, built under the company name Dart Manufacturing. Lane purchased and sold the Dart at Port Columbus before the war.

When World War II began the Navy took over all of Port Columbus to improve the war effort and Lane was forced to move his business to The Ohio State University's new Don Scott Field north of Columbus.

He decided that he could support the war effort best by training pilots for the Navy there at Don Scott. He was awarded a contract by the Navy to train their future pilots in a program named the War Training Service (W.T.S.). His W.T.S. operation trained hundreds of pilots for the Navy during the war.[331]

After the war Foster Lane moved back to Port Columbus to continue a very successful and long standing company. He died in 1995 at the age of 92.

Lane Aviation is still in the aviation business at Port Columbus and as an FBO continues to serve pilots and their aviation needs decades after its first beginnings.

Alex A. Boudreaux

Photo of the Alex A. Boudreaux.
Photo courtesy of Columbus Dispatch.

Alex A. Boudreaux had a long and distinguished career in aviation. He was born in Louisiana in 1920 and at age five he was carrying water and gasoline to barnstorming pilots who were landing in local fields. Some

The Building of an Airport: Port Columbus

grateful pilots would give short flights to show their appreciation to him. He fell in love with aviation and constantly dreamed of becoming a pilot.

As he grew older he enrolled in college at Xavier University in New Orleans and completed two years of education there. When World War II began he enlisted in the U.S. Army Air Corps Reserves. He was soon called to active duty as an aviation cadet in February of 1943 to serve with the now famous Tuskegee Airmen in Alabama. He was a member of the training Class of 43J.

He had almost completed his pilot training when, without explanation, it was called to a halt. He then began training and served in radio communications at Tuskegee. This soon led him to become an Air Traffic Controller. After leaving the military he worked as a civilian Air Traffic Controller at Lockbourne AAF for three years.

Thus began his 33-year career as an air traffic controller and the first black controller in the United States.

He and his wife Mary moved to Columbus where he served for 30 years as an Air Traffic Controller at Port Columbus. During those years he earned his pilot's certificates and held commercial, instrument and flight instructor ratings. He flew often from Port Columbus and was well known there among those involved in aviation.

During his life he became a lifetime member of the Ohio Chapter of Tuskegee Airmen, member of Motts Military Museum and a founding member of the Ohio Museum of Flight at Port Columbus.

In 2005 he was inducted into the Ohio Veterans Hall of Fame and in 2007 received the Congressional Gold Medal. He and his wife were married for 56 years. He died at age 90 in Port Columbus.[332]

Robert F. Kirk

Francis "Jack" Bolton
Port Columbus Airport Manager 1945-1968

Photo of Jack Bolton (center) standing in front of Port
Columbus' new tower being constructed.
Photo courtesy of Columbus Dispatch.

The Building of an Airport: Port Columbus

Photo of the Jack Bolton sitting at his desk at Port Columbus Tower.
Photo courtesy of Columbus Dispatch.

Francis "Jack" Bolton was born in 1919 at Newark, Ohio. He went to Columbus in 1937 to study at The Ohio State University. After studying there for three years he took a job working in the experimental department of Curtiss-Wright Corporation in Columbus.

When World War II began he joined the Navy and served as a maintenance officer. He also served during the war as an air combat intelligence officer. At the end of the war he was stationed at Port Columbus assigned to work on business issues between the Navy and the city.[333]

In 1945 Bolton was named Superintendent of Port Columbus Airport. At only 26 years old he was the nation's youngest superintendent at a major national airport. He achieved important milestones at Port Columbus during his time there but one of the most important ones was that he became an expert on airport snow removal.[334]

During his tenure Port Columbus was closed only once because of snow and ice during the 1950 blizzard. Bolton was able to keep Port Columbus open during the rest of his 23 years in charge.

Another major accomplishment by Bolton was that he was able to qualify Port Columbus to become an International Airport.

Bolton made his residence on airport property and made himself on call 24 hours a day and seven days a week. His intense call to duty may have contributed to his tragic early death at an age of only 49 years old.

Bolton is remembered with a citation inside the walls of Port Columbus which recalls he had a single-minded devotion to the cause of aviation.

When a new airport, TZR, was opened in 1970 for general aviation, the city also honored Jack Bolton posthumously for his aviation contributions by dedicating the new airport as Bolton Field.

The Building of an Airport: Port Columbus

Geraldine "Jerrie" Mock
First Woman to Fly Solo Around the World

Photo of Jerrie Mock.
Photo courtesy of Columbus Dispatch.

Geraldine "Jerrie" Fredritz Mock was born in 1925 at Newark, Ohio. She made her first flight with her father in a Ford Tri-Motor when she was only five years old. After she completed high school she went to The Ohio State University and became one of the first female aeronautical engineering students.

She married Russell Mock who was a pilot and she enjoyed flying cross-country trips with him. When she was 32 years old she began training to become a pilot. She obtained her pilot's license and went on to complete an instrument rating. She wanted to see the world so she began preparing for and planning an around the world flight.[335]

She had competition for the trip in that Joan Smith was also planning such a trip in her twin engine Piper. Jerrie held fund raising activities with her husband to help finance the trip.

Jerrie selected a 1953 Cessna 180 single engine aircraft for her expected round the world trip. She named her aircraft the Spirit of Columbus. Previous attempts to complete the journey had all been unsuccessful including that of Amelia Earhart 27 years earlier.

The Cessna 180 was modified to add additional radios for navigation and communication. Additional fuel tanks we also added to the aircraft to add 183 gallons of fuel. This provided a range of about 3,500 miles, however it also added 1,098 pounds of fuel weight. Even with a reduction in the normal weight of her aircraft by removing normal items, her plane was 900 pounds over gross weight. The FAA granted her a special ferry permit to fly in the overloaded condition. She took a small typewriter and wrote articles for the Columbus Dispatch along the way.[336]

Jerrie planned very well from a navigational standpoint working with others to gain from their knowledge and experience. With her paperwork correct she began her flight from Port Columbus, Ohio, eastbound on March 19, 1964.

Her trip took her to Bermuda; Santa Maria, Azores; Casablanca, Morocco; Annaba, Algeria; Tripoli, Libya; Almaza AFB and Cairo, Egypt; Dhahran, Saudi Arabia; Karachi, Pakistan; Delhi and Calcutta, India; Bangkok, Thailand; overflew Vietnam; Manila, Philippines; Guam; Wake Island; Honolulu, Hawaii; Oakland, California; Tucson, Arizona; and finally back to Port Columbus landing on April 17, 1964. The trip took her a total of 29 days, 11 hours and 59 minutes. She flew a total of 23,103 miles on her round the world journey. She became the first woman to fly solo around the world.[337]

On May 4, 1964 President Lyndon Johnson presented Jerrie with the Federal Aviation Administration's Exceptional Service Decoration. She also became the first woman to be awarded the FAA's Louis Bleriot Silver Medal.[338]

The Building of an Airport: Port Columbus

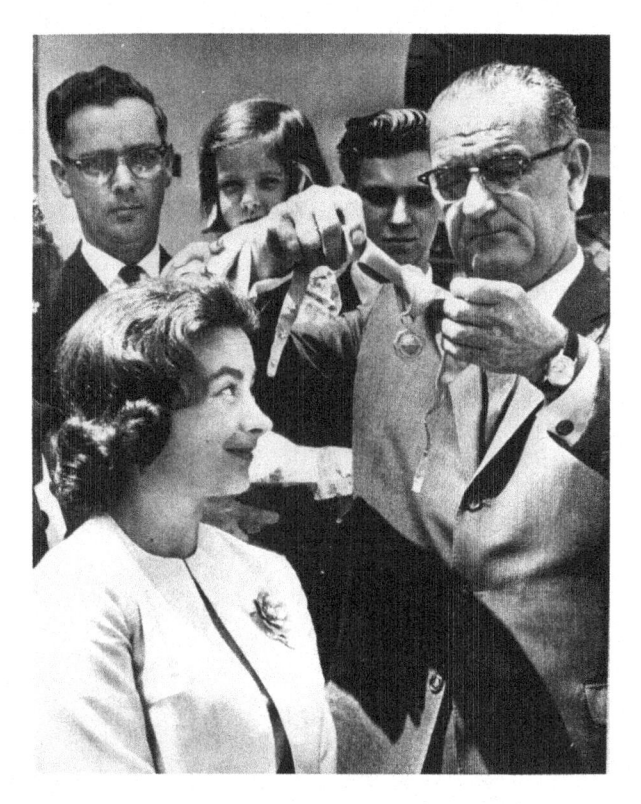

Photo of Jerrie Mock receiving the Federal Aviation Administration's Exceptional Service Decoration from President Lyndon Johnson in 1964. Photo courtesy National Air and Space Museum, Smithsonian Institution, NASM-2B19530.

Jerrie went on to fly other long distance worldwide trips and receive many official world aviation records and honors.

The "Spirit of Columbus" was purchased from her and displayed in the National Air and Space Museum, Udvar-Hazy Center.

Jerrie passed away in September, 2014 at the age of 88.

Captain Edward A. Gillespie

Photo of Ed Gillespie as Lt. Commander in the United States Navy.
Photo courtesy of Scott Gillespie, Executor of Ed Gillespie Estate.

Captain "Ed" Gillespie was born in Ann Arbor, Michigan in 1928. He started a love affair with flying that began at a very young age. At the age of 12 he flew with a neighbor who was a photographer and owned an aircraft. He took young Ed up flying with him. While his neighbor was taking pictures, Ed flew the airplane and held it steady for better photos.[339]

Ed saved his money and took flying lessons. He soloed in 1944 at age 16. He completed his private pilot's certificate a year later.

While he was still in high school he enlisted in the Navy Aviation Midshipman Program. He continued his education in the field of engineering at both Syracuse and Western Michigan Universities. In 1948 he began Navy Preflight Pilot Training and after pilot training, worked on and became carrier qualified. He flew a selection of different aircraft until he was selected to attend jet transition training. He completed jet qualification and was assigned fleet duty flying the Navy's new carrier-based F2H Banshee jet fighter aircraft with the VF-11, *The Red Rippers* one of the first Navy jet squadrons. He spent three years in this assignment, which took him off the coast of Korea during the Korean War. He flew 80 combat missions over Korea supporting ground troops in contact fighting the Communists.[340]

Photo of F2H-2 Banshee, an aircraft that was flown by Ed Gillespie over Korea while in the Navy.
Official U.S. Navy Photo – Public Domain.

Ed built a lot of flying time in the F2H and became a technical director for a number of Navy training films. During filming as he was flying and advising in the F2H he got into a spin trying to follow the film director's instructions. He fought to exit the spin until finally he was successful just 500 feet above the water.

After his fleet duty, Ed was offered a choice between joining the Blue Angels and attending the Navy's Test Pilot School. He decided to take the offer of attending the test pilot training and graduated in 1954.

Ed left active duty in 1956 and began work as a test pilot for North American Aviation in Ohio. However, he remained in the Navy Reserves until 1982 and retired with 36 years of service and the rank of Captain. He went on to become North American's Chief Test Pilot. During his years there he flew many well-known high performance aircraft. He retired from North American in 1988 but continued to fly and test aircraft.

Photo of Ed Gillespie at a 2002-2003 aircraft Fly-In.
Photo courtesy of Scott Gillespie, Executor of Ed Gillespie Estate.

Ed Gillespie's Passion for the Port Columbus Administration-Passenger Terminal

The Administration-Passenger terminal that had been constructed in 1929 experienced many years of changes that took place in aviation throughout the years. It had been through World War II and experienced modifications including many physical additions to the airport. It became part of the beginning of airline passenger service across the United States with T.A.T.'s transcontinental service in 1929. Passengers from the Pennsylvania Railroad Terminal passed through its building to board the first all metal airplane made in the U.S., the Ford Tri-Motor. It had experienced first hand a long list of aviation giants utilizing its facility including Charles Lindbergh and Amelia Earhart. But now it was facing its biggest challenge.

The city of Columbus decided the terminal had out lived its usefulness and decided it needed to be torn down. The city forgot that once it had been a magnificent building. Its octagonal control tower alone set it apart from all other control towers. It had an architectural design that was, with its tower, stunning! The Columbus Chapter of American Institute of Architecture in 1975 referred to the terminal's history and beginnings as "unique."

But the decision was made to tear the building down. However, Ed Gillespie, who had been part of the tower's long history, had other ideas about the building's future. He worked with the city and was able to obtain a 40-year lease on the terminal. It consisted of an initial 20-year lease with four 5-year renewal options. It is believed the lease began in the spring of 1984. Ed began the restoration immediately and set about the task of returning the terminal to its original condition. It was a large job because the building was a mess![341]

The basement was flooded, the interior was rotting from the leaking roof that had been repaired so many times it was a disaster. Gillespie, along with many friends and volunteers, worked on the project for about 48 months with Gillespie investing $600,000 in the restoration.

First of all the old additions to the original building had to be removed. This in itself was a major undertaking. Yet to Ed Gillespie "the building was a thing of beauty" and it represented an important section of aviation history. Of all of Ed Gillespie's aviation achievements, and there are many, perhaps his greatest was his huge effort to restore and preserve the Port Columbus Administration Passenger building for the citizens of Columbus and for the aviation legacy of T.A.T.'s Transcontinental Airline Passenger service of 1929.

Robert F. Kirk

Photo of Administration-Passenger building before and
after Ed Gillespie's restoration in 1984-88.
Photo courtesy of Scott Gillespie, Executor of Ed Gillespie Estate.

The Building of an Airport: Port Columbus

Photo of work to repair the roof on the Port Columbus Terminal. 150 tons of concrete and sand had to be removed to begin the repair to the roof. Photo courtesy of Scott Gillespie, Executor of Ed Gillespie Estate.

Robert F. Kirk

Photo of men working to build a foundation for the new roof on the Terminal.
Photo courtesy of Scott Gillespie, Executor of Ed Gillespie Estate.

The Building of an Airport: Port Columbus

Photo of work to place a rubber covering on the roof to keep it waterproof.
The man standing at far right with his shirt off is Ed Gillespie.
Photo courtesy of Scott Gillespie, Executor of Ed Gillespie Estate.

John Herschel Glenn Jr.

Photo of John Glenn receiving an award from NASA.
Photo courtesy of NASA.

John Glenn was born on July 18, 1921 in Cambridge, Ohio. He attended both primary and secondary schools in New Concord, Ohio. He went to Muskingum College and earned his Bachelor of Science degree in engineering there. In March 1942 Glenn joined the Naval Aviation Cadet Program and after graduation from the school earned his commission and his pilot's wings. With additional training he joined the Marine Fighter Squadron 155 and was assigned to the Marshall Islands. He spent a year there and flew 59 combat missions during World War II. He flew the F4U Corsair fighter.[342]

It is a little known piece of history that an already famous aviator was also flying and fighting for the war effort. This famous aviator was Charles Lindbergh who was the first person to fly solo across the Atlantic in 1927. He was now in the South Pacific flying combat missions in the F4U and also helping Marine and Navy pilots learn to better fly the F4U. An interview with John Glenn years later tells about this important gem of history.

It was funny, later on, then during World War II, I knew Lindbergh a little bit, not really well. When we were flying the F4Us, the Corsairs. Later on in WW II the Corsairs had a lot of trouble…They had worked most of the bugs out of the airplane, and he was coming around to the different squadrons to demonstrate it…It was a little hard to handle. But there was enough problems with it, and it was a suspect enough airplane that [Charles] Lindbergh; then working for United Aircraft actually came around flying a Corsair to different squadrons to give some instruction on the new characteristics…once the…Corsair had been corrected. He came and stayed at our squadron for 1…3-4 days and so we got to know him. Then later on,…overseas in combat out in the Marshall Islands, he… actually flew a couple of missions with us out there, we were doing actual live bombing on enemy positions.[343]

Charles Lindbergh reported several of his combat missions in his book – *The Wartime Journals of Charles A. Lindbergh*. He spoke of one of his combat missions with the F4U.

We swing around into position. Major Armstrong noses down. Five seconds later I follow. The building is squarely in my sight; but Armstrong's plane is in the way—don't want to shoot so close to him. His tracers are striking his target and ricocheting back up off the ground. I am at 2,000 feet now, but he is still in the way. I keep the building in my sight and hold fire—roof, palm trees, and ground rushing up at me…Armstrong pulls up. I press the trigger. Long streams of tracers bury themselves in the roof and wall. Everything is still lifeless. The ground is close. I level out over the treetops. It was a short burst, but most of the bullets went home.[344]

Lindbergh went on to fly at least 14 combat missions in the F4U Corsair as well as many in the P-38 Lightning.

Photo of Charles Lindbergh with Three Marine
Pilots in the South Pacific during WW II.
Photo courtesy of National Air and Space Museum,
Smithsonian Institution, NASM-9A08349.

The Building of an Airport: Port Columbus

Photo of Charles Lindbergh in the cockpit of a Vought F4U Corsair getting ready to takeoff on a combat mission in the South Pacific during WW II. Photo courtesy of National Air and Space Museum, Smithsonian Institution, NASM-9A08348.

It wasn't recorded that Lindbergh and Glenn flew Corsairs on bombing missions together but it is note worthy that such two great aviation heroes were flying combat missions in the Marshall Islands at the same time during World War II.

During WW II Glenn flew 59 combat missions and during the Korean War he flew 63 combat missions with Marine Fighter Squadron 311. Glenn later flew as an exchange pilot with the Air Force and flew 27 combat missions in the F-86 Sabre Jet. Glenn was credited with the downing of three MIG fighters.

After the Korean War Glenn went to Navy Test Pilot School. In July 1957 he set a transcontinental speed record flying the F8U Crusader from Los Angeles to New York in a time of 3 hours and 23 minutes. It is also interesting to note that Lindbergh was also part of a transcontinental record in 1929 with the Transcontinental Airline Transport (T.A.T.) passenger service that left Los Angeles and arrived in New York in just 48 hours.

John Glenn went on to have an amazing career and life. He became one of the first original NASA astronauts and the first American to orbit the Earth. He eventually resigned from the astronaut program and soon after retired from the Marine Corps.

Within a few years he ran for and was elected to the United States Senate. He went on to serve a total of four six-year terms as Senator from Ohio.

In 1998 Glenn returned to space on the Discovery Shuttle flight. That made him the oldest person to go into space. He was 77 years old.

On May 25, 2016 the Ohio General Assembly passed a bill renaming the Port Columbus International Airport to the John Glenn Columbus International Airport. John Glenn passed away on December 8, 2016 at the age of 95.

DID YOU KNOW?

Little Bits of Intriguing Information on the History of Port Columbus

1. Did you know that the first air shipment of goods for Port Columbus was delivered in July 1929?

It was the canvas used to cover the T.A.T. walkway awnings.

2. Did you know that Port Columbus was predicted to turn a profit after starting operation in 1929? That prediction did turn true but it had to wait a few years before doing so because of the consequences of the Great Depression and World War II.

However, in its 15th year it did turn its first profit and continued to do so for many years.

3. Did you know that the famous first transcontinental airlines known as the Transcontinental Air Transport Company, T.A.T. merged with other airlines, Maddux Airlines and Western Air Express, to form the well-known airline of T.W.A. that remained in business for many years?

4. Did you know that the U.S., in anticipation of war with Germany, began to become the "arsenal of democracy?" In so doing in July 1940 approved the building of a Curtiss-Wright Aircraft Plant at Port Columbus. The plant was completed, after construction began, in just 147 days. It was in full production by late 1941.

5. Did you know that the first year of its operation in 1929, Port Columbus had 11,000 people fly as passengers?

6. Did you know that in 1938 the Public Works Administration completed the east/west runway to Port Columbus and in 1941 the Navy lengthened it to 5,000 feet?

7. Did you know that Curtiss-Wright produced over 5,200 SB2C HellDiver Dive Bombers and over 570 SO3C Observation aircraft for the Navy at Port Columbus from 1940 to 1950?[345]

Photo of Curtiss SB2C HellDiver assigned to the USS Yorktown flying strike missions on Iwo Jima in February 1945.
Photo Official U.S. Navy photograph, Public Domain.

The Building of an Airport: Port Columbus

8. Did you know that the U.S. Navy took over operation of Port Columbus in 1941, built a hangar and established a Navy operation there until after the war? The Navy released control of Port Columbus in 1946.

9. Did you know that North American Aviation, Inc. took over the plant from Curtiss-Wright in November 1950 following the start of the Korean War?

10. Did you know that from 1952 through 1977 North American Aviation produced almost 4,400 aircraft? Some of these aircraft included the F-86, F-100, and the OV-10 for the Air Force.[346]

11. Did you know that total plant production at Curtiss-Wright and North American Aviation saw the production of over 13,000 aircraft including the B-1 Bomber?[347]

12. Did you know that two new Port Columbus Air Traffic Control towers were opened in 1954 and in 2004? This was because of the growth of the airport air traffic.

13. Did you know that Port Columbus built a new terminal building in September 1958?

14. Did you know that Trans World Airlines (TWA) began the first Pure Jet service at Port Columbus in 1961? TWA utilized propeller aircraft up until this time.[348]

Robert F. Kirk

Photo - Aerial view of TWA DC-2 passenger aircraft parked at Port Columbus Administration-Passenger Terminal in the late 1930's. Photo courtesy of Captain Don Peters' Collection.

The Building of an Airport: Port Columbus

15. Did you know that in 1965 Port Columbus became an International Airport?

16. Did you know that with the Port Columbus' 50th anniversary the original Administration-Passenger Terminal was added to the National Register of Historic Places?

17. Did you know that in February 2000 Port Columbus completed it largest capital improvement project for a cost of $92 million?

18. Did you know that TWA, which evolved from the original T.A.T., ended 72 years of continuous service and was purchased by American Airlines in 2001?

19. Did you know that the 90th anniversary of the old Port Columbus Airport is this year on July 8, 2019?

20. Did you know that the name of Port Columbus International Airport was changed to the John Glenn Columbus International Airport on May 15, 2016?

21. Did you know that Louise Thaden who won the first Women's Air Derby was also the first woman pilot to achieve a pilot's license in Ohio even though she was from Arkansas?

22. Did you know that Jerrie Mock, who was the first woman to fly solo around the world received very little recognition for what she accomplished? Nothing like that of Amelia Earhart who failed in her attempt. Jerrie went on to fly to destinations worldwide with little fan fair.

ENDNOTES

1. *Commander Davis & Aide are Killed,* Columbus Dispatch, April 26, 1927.
2. Thomas Kessner, *The Flight of the Century,* Oxford University Press, 2010, p. 61-65.
3. *Air Conquest of Oceans Exacts Mighty Toll,* Columbus Dispatch, Sept 8, 1927.
4. *Plan Wide Search for Fliers,* Columbus Dispatch, May 10, 1927.
5. Air Conquest of Oceans, *Op. cit.,* Sept 8, 1927.
6. Ibid.
7. *U.S. Aviators Ready for Ocean Flight,* Columbus Evening Dispatch, May 13, 1927.
8. Ibid. Kessner, *op. cit.,* p. 74.
9. *Start of U.S. Trans-Ocean Planes Delayed by Weather,* Columbus Evening Dispatch, May 14, 1927.
10. *Lindbergh Reaches Nova Scotia,* Columbus Evening Dispatch, May 20, 1927.
11. Kessner, *op. cit.,* p. 64.
12. Charles A. Lindbergh, *"WE",* Grosset & Dunlap, NY, 1927, p. 201.
13. Ibid.
14. Ibid. p. 206.
15. Ibid. p. 198.
16. *"WE": The Epic of the Air,* Chapter 23, Columbus Dispatch, Feb. 2, 1928.
17. Lindbergh *op. cit.,* p. 219.
18. Ibid. p. 205.
19. *World Acclamation Goes to Lindbergh for Epochal Non-Stop Flight to Paris,* Columbus Dispatch, May 22, 1927.

20   *Lindbergh Reaches France After Epochal Flight Across Atlantic,* Columbus Evening Dispatch, May 21, 1927.
21   World Acclamation Goes to Lindbergh, *op. cit.*
22   *President Doumergue confers Highest Possible Order Upon Young America Flying Ace,* Columbus Dispatch, May 23, 1927.
23   *Huge Crowds Greet Flier in Brussels,* Columbus Evening Dispatch, May 28, 1927.
24   *Lindbergh May Return Home on Destroyer,* Columbus Evening Dispatch, May 24, 1927.
25   *Lindbergh at End of Tour,* Has No Plans for Future, Columbus Dispatch, October 24, 1927.
26   *Lindy has 25,000 miles; late just once,* Columbus Dispatch, September 21, 1927.
27   *Eight Leading U.S. Aviators are in Boston,* Columbus Dispatch, July 23, 1927.
28   *Nation to Pay Lindbergh Highest Honor,* Columbus Dispatch, March 16, 1928.
29   *Lindbergh to Arrive in St. Louis Friday,* Columbus Dispatch, June 15, 1927.
30   *Airplane Output is Greatly Increased,* Columbus Dispatch, August 18, 1927.
31   *Upward Trend of Commercial Aviation in Last Year,* Columbus Dispatch, July 19, 1927.
32   *Lindbergh – Spirit of Columbus,* Columbus Dispatch, July 11, 1927.
33   *Col. Lindbergh Thrills Columbus,* Columbus Dispatch, June 17, 1927.
34   *Aviation – Airshow Plans Grow,* Columbus Dispatch, July 24, 1927.
35   Ibid.
36   Lindbergh *op. cit.,* July 11, 1927.
37   *Aero Club Has Helped Columbus,* The Columbus Sunday Dispatch, July 7, 1929.
38   *Stork _004*
39   Aero Club Has Helped Columbus *op. cit.*
40   Ibid.
41   Ibid.
42   Ibid.

43 Stork _013
44 *Life Memberships Are Selling Fast,* Columbus Sunday Dispatch, Aug 12, 1928.
45 Stork _017, _030, _034.
46 *Declare Lack of Airports Hold Back Aviation,* Columbus Dispatch, September 21, 1927.
47 Ibid.
48 Ibid.
49 Ibid.
50 Ibid.
51 Declare Lack of Airports Hold Back Aviation, *op. cit.*
52 *City Air Board Named to Direct Flying Activities,* Columbus Dispatch, June 21, 1927.
53 *Air Groups to Plan Greeting for Fliers,* Columbus Dispatch, June 22, 1927.
54 Ibid.
55 *Lindbergh Expected in Dayton at 5 p.m.,* Columbus Dispatch, June 22, 1927.
56 Ibid.
57 *Lindbergh's Plan Heralded as Big Aid to Aviation,* Columbus Dispatch, June 25, 1927.
58 Ibid.
59 *Immediate Need of New Airport Voiced by Board,* Columbus Dispatch, July 6, 1927.
60 Ibid.
61 Ibid.
62 *Economic Benefit of New Airport to City Stress,* Columbus Dispatch, October 2, 1927.
63 Ibid.
64 Ibid.
65 *$425,000 Issue For Airport to Appear on Ballot,* Columbus Dispatch, September 7, 1927.
66 Ibid.
67 *Airboard Seeks Bond Issue For Aviation Field,* Columbus Dispatch, September 3, 1927.

68   *40 Airports Operate in Ohio*, Columbus Dispatch, October 23, 1927.
69   *Lindbergh Credit in Air-Mail Growth*, Columbus Dispatch, October 30, 1927.
70   *Columbus – Bond Issue Defeated*, The Chronicle-Telegram, Elyria, Ohio, November 9, 1927.
71   *Crew of 40 with 20 Additional Passengers Aboard*, Columbus Evening Dispatch, October 11, 1928.
72   Ibid.
73   *German Dirigible Ready to Start Ocean Flight Tuesday*, Columbus Dispatch, October 6, 1928.
74   Crew of 40, *op. cit.*
75   Don M. Casto III, Conversation with author, June 5, 2018.
76   *Mrs. Clara Adams, the First American Woman to Cross the Atlantic by Dirigible*, The Evening Tribune, Marysville, Ohio, October 25, 1928.
77   *Columbus Placed on Graf Zeppelin's Tour*, Columbus Evening Dispatch, October 20, 1928.
78   *Friedrichshafen Germany TO at Lakehurst, N.J.*, New York Times, October 30, 1928.
79   Ibid.
80   Ibid.
81   *Exact Course of Air Liner is not Known*, The Evening Independent, Massillon, Ohio, October 30, 1928.
82   *Great Trip Says Don Casto of Zeppelin Ride*, Columbus Evening Dispatch, November 1, 1928.
83   Ibid.
84   Ibid.
85   Ibid.
86   Ibid.
87   *Log of the Graf Zeppelin*, Don M. Casto Foundation Scrapbook, 1928.
88   *Cotton Bale in Cargo Hailed*, New York Times, October 30, 1928.
89   *Zeppelin Has Reached France on Return Trip to Home Port*, The Evening Tribune, Maryville, Ohio, October 31, 1928.

90 *Zep. Completes Longest Eastward Ocean Flight,* Columbus Evening Dispatch, November 1, 1928.
91 Ibid.
92 *City of Columbus Plans New Drive for City Airport,* Columbus Evening Dispatch, May 16, 1928.
93 *New Need For City Airport Voiced,* Columbus Dispatch, March 25, 1928.
94 *Air-Train System Soon to be Reality,* Columbus Dispatch, May 15, 1928.
95 Ibid.
96 Ibid.
97 Ibid. (Also see letter from Karl E. Burr who was working to finalize plans for T.A.T. to make Columbus it east most terminus. The Columbus Chamber of Commerce was actively involved in making the airport a reality.)
98 Ibid.
99 Ibid.
100 *City Selected As Transfer Point in Rail-Air Line,* Columbus Dispatch, March 22, 1928.
101 Ibid.
102 Ibid.
103 *Auto Manufacturer Takes Whirl in Colonel Lindbergh's Spirit of St. Louis,* Columbus Dispatch, August 12, 1927. & *Lindbergh Takes Henry Ford on His First Ride In An AirPlane,* Columbus Dispatch, August 13, 1927. See also William T. Larkins, *The Ford Tri-Motor 1926-1992,* Schiffer, 160.
104 *Ford Flivver Airplane #1, 1926,* Henry Ford Aviation, The Henry Ford Collections, 2019.
105 City Selected As Transfer Point, *op. cit.*
106 Ibid.
107 *To Announce Site in Two Weeks,* Columbus Dispatch, July 9, 1928.
108 *Select Columbus as Eastern Air Terminal for T.A.T.,* Columbus Dispatch, April 1, 1928.
109 *Transport Co. Official Likes Local "Port" Site,* Columbus Dispatch, September 17, 1928.

110 *118 Airports Built in 1928 Records Show,* The Columbus Sunday Dispatch, December 16, 1928.
111 Ibid.
112 *Aviation Appointment of New Air Board is Aim at City Progress,* The Columbus Sunday Dispatch, June 24, 1928.
113 *Council to be Asked to Add Ten Members,* The Columbus Sunday Dispatch, June 17, 1928.
114 *Aviation: Airport Survey Under Way Here,* The Columbus Sunday Dispatch, June 3, 1928.
115 City of Columbus Plans New Drive, *op. cit.*
116 *New Air Board is Named,* Columbus Evening Dispatch, June 21, 1928.
117 Ibid.
118 New Need For City Airport Voiced, *op. cit.*
119 *Airport Commission Plans Get Approval of Lindberg,* The Columbus Sunday Dispatch, August 12, 1928.
120 Ibid.
121 Ibid.
122 Ibid.
123 Ibid.
124 Ibid.
125 *Committee of 300 Organize Selves to Urge Approval of City Airport,* The Columbus Sunday Dispatch, September 23, 1928.
126 *Aviation: Public Sentiment Favors Municipal Airport Project,* The Columbus Sunday Dispatch, May 27, 1928.
127 Ibid.
128 Ibid.
129 *Promise New Industry If Airport is Approved,* The Columbus Sunday Dispatch, November 4, 1928.
130 Ibid.
131 Ibid.
132 *What You Would Know About Columbus Airport Is Answered Here,* The Columbus Sunday Dispatch, September 30, 1928.
133 *Council Favors $850,000 Airport,* Columbus Evening Dispatch, September 6, 1928.

134 *Address of Lindbergh's "Just U.S.A. for While"*, Waterloo Iowa Courier, July 10, 1929.
135 *Aviation: Airport Bond Issue to be Placed Before Voters,* The Columbus Dispatch, September 9, 1928.
136 Ibid.
137 Ibid.
138 *Flying in Short Has Ceased to Being a Novelty,* Columbus Dispatch, Sept 30, 1928.
139 *A Ford Tri-Motored All-Metal Monoplane Will Carry Passengers,* Columbus Dispatch, September 18, 1928.
140 *Crowds Seek to Ride in Tri-Motored Plane,* The Columbus Dispatch, September 24, 1928.
141 Ibid.
142 *Says Airport Will Bring New Industries,* Columbus Dispatch, September 19, 1928.
143 *Says City is Natural Choice for Airport,* Columbus Dispatch, September 22, 1928.
144 Ibid.
145 *Transport Co. Official Likes Local "Port" Site,* Columbus Dispatch, September 17, 1928.
146 *The City Bulletin, Vol. XII I, No. 54, December 31, 1927.*
147 *Now Up to the People,* Columbus Dispatch, September 28, 1928.
148 Conversation with Don M. Casto III, *op. cit.*
149 *German Experts to Give Advice,* The Columbus Sunday Dispatch, November 18, 1928.
150 Ibid.
151 Ibid.
152 Ibid.
153 Ibid.
154 *Zeppelin Overcame Squall That Wrecked Shenandoah, Casto Says, of Air Trip,* Columbus Evening Dispatch, Nov. 14, 1928.
155 *Airport is Approved,* Columbus Dispatch, October 13, 1928.
156 *Airport Bond Issue is Only One on Ballot,* The Columbus Sunday Dispatch, November 4, 1928.
157 *This is the Airport Ballot: How & Why to Vote For It.* Columbus Dispatch, November 5, 1928.

158 *Fear of Travel: Plane vs Rail,* Columbus Dispatch, September 23, 1928.
159 Ibid.
160 Ibid.
161 *Dispatch Rural Routes to Be Covered by Airplanes,* The Columbus Sunday Dispatch, October 28, 1928.
162 *Airport to be Opened as Soon as is Possible,* Columbus Evening Dispatch, November 7, 1928.
163 Ibid.
164 Ibid.
165 *Airport Will Cost Less Than Others of Its Type,* October 25, 1928.
166 Airport to be Opened, *op. cit.*
167 *Airport Site Near Army Depot Chosen on Approval of Lindbergh and Experts,* Columbus Evening Dispatch, September 10, 1928.
168 Ibid.
169 *Lady Lindy is Charming and Knows Her Airplanes,* Columbus Evening Dispatch, November 19, 1928.
170 Airport to be Opened, *op. cit.*
171 Ibid.
172 *First Citizens Trust Company Ad,* Columbus Dispatch, Nov 9, 1928.
173 *Air Heart Here,* The Columbus Sunday Dispatch, July 7, 1929.
174 *Crew at Work Surveying Airport Site,* Columbus Dispatch, November 7, 1928.
175 *No Field in World is Comparable to Columbus Airport,* The Columbus Sunday Dispatch, July 7, 1929.
176 Ibid.
177 Ibid.
178 Ibid.
179 *New Airport to be Finest Inland Aviation Center in United States, Is Claimed,* The Columbus Sunday Dispatch, November 11, 1928.
180 Ibid.
181 Ibid.
182 Ibid.
183 *Airport Site is Surveyed,* Columbus Evening Dispatch, November 9, 1928.
184 *No Field in World is Comparable, op. cit.*

185 *City Engineer is Preparing to Lay Out Airport,* Columbus Evening Dispatch, November 1, 1928.
186 *Columbus to Have Airport Division of City Government,* The Sandusky Register, Ohio, December 9, 1928.
187 No Field in World is Comparable, *op. cit.*
188 *Letter by Herbert Baumer,* The Ohio State University, Columbus, Ohio, September 4, 1962.
189 Stork _353
190 *Solons May Condemn Land for Airport,* The Herald-Star, Steubenville, Ohio, November 27, 1928.
191 *Speed in Building T.A.T. Hangar,* Columbus Dispatch, July 7, 1929.
192 *Columbus…America's Air Capital,* Columbus Dispatch, July 7, 1929.
193 *Stork _315*
194 Ibid.
195 Stork _353
196 Stork _288
197 Ibid.
198 Ibid.
199 Ibid.
200 *All Hangar Leases Are to be for Five Years,* Columbus Dispatch, March, 1929.
201 *5:1 Approval of Bond Issue in Nov. 1928 for $850,000,* The Columbus Citizen, November 7, 1928.
202 *Port Columbus As It Will Appear,* Columbus Sunday Dispatch, November 4, 1928.
203 *Office Building at Airport,* The Columbus Citizen, February 6, 1929.
204 Stork _292
205 Ibid.
206 Ibid.
207 Office Building at Airport, *op. cit.*
208 Stork _292
209 Stork _308
210 Stork _292
211 Ibid.

212 Office Building at Airport, *op. cit.*
213 *Office Building at Airport*, Columbus Evening Dispatch, Sept 10, 1928.
214 *No Port Comparable With City's Terminal*, Columbus Sunday Dispatch, July 7, 1929.
215 *The Middle States Construction Company*, Columbus Dispatch, July7, 1929.
216 Speed in Building T.A.T. Hangar, *op. cit.*
217 *Seven Hangars – Spaces Taken On Air Field*, Columbus Sunday Dispatch, July 7, 1929.
218 Stork _157
219 No Port Comparable, *op. cit.*
220 *Airport Bonds Will Be Sold in December*, Columbus Dispatch, November 15, 1928.
221 Stork _293
222 Stork _037
223 Ibid.
224 Stork _038
225 Ibid.
226 Stork _293
227 Ibid.
228 Stork _039
229 Stork _090
230 Stork _038
231 Stork _102
232 Stork _232
233 Stork _293
234 Stork _118
235 Ibid.
236 Stork _038
237 Ibid.
238 *Drainage System at Airport Simplified*, Columbus Dispatch, November 10, 1928.
239 Ibid.
240 *New Problems in Construction of Airport*, Columbus Sunday Dispatch, July 7, 1929.

241	Stork _118
242	Stork _232
243	New Problems in Construction of Airport, *op. cit.*
244	Stork _118
245	Stork _290
246	Stork _084
247	Stork _351
248	Ibid.
249	Ibid.
250	Stork _387
251	*The Ohio State Engineer*, Editorial, February, 1929.
252	118 Airports Built in 1928 Records Show, *op. cit.*
253	Stork _118
254	Stork _039
255	Stork _041
256	Stork _065
257	Stork _314
258	Stork _355
259	Stork _381
260	Stork _232
261	*Lighting Plans for Airport Are Drafted,* Columbus Dispatch, November 15, 1928.
262	Ibid.
263	Stork _378
264	Stork _071
265	Stork _293
266	Stork _370
267	Stork _040
268	Stork _293
269	Stork _072
270	Stork _293
271	Stork _080
272	Stork _293
273	Stork _315
274	Stork _314

275 *Transcontinental Route Guarded by Elaborate System of Weather Bureaus,* Columbus Sunday Dispatch, July 7, 1929.
276 Ibid.
277 Stork _315
278 Ibid.
279 Stork _387
280 Stork _384
281 *Air Traffic Cost 47 Lives in Six Months,* Columbus Dispatch, October 23, 1927.
282 Ibid.
283 *The Ohio State Engineer*, Editorial, p.18, November, 1928.
284 Ibid.
285 *Transcontinental Air Line First Conceived in Club Dining Rooms,* Columbus Sunday Dispatch, July 7, 1929.
286 Ibid.
287 *Aviation,* McGraw-Hill, July 6, 1929.
288 Ibid.
289 Ibid.
290 Robert F. Kirk, *Flying the Lindbergh Line: Then and Now,* AuthorHouse Publishing, 2012.
291 Aviation, *op. cit.*
292 *Lindbergh Inspects T.A.T. Western Route,* Las Vegas Daily Optic, N.M., February 18, 1929.
293 *Columbus Air History May Well Date From Today,* Columbus Dispatch, July 7, 1929.
294 Ibid.
295 *Ford Terms Air and Rail Alliance Historic Event,* Columbus Evening Dispatch, July 8, 1929.
296 Ibid.
297 *Air to Co-Operate With Other Methods of Travel,* Columbus Sunday Dispatch, July 7, 1929.
298 *Fleet of Eight Planes to Arrive – Will Stage Night Display,* Columbus Evening Dispatch, July 5, 1929.
299 Ibid.
300 *Miss Earhart Conquers Ocean,* Columbus Evening Dispatch, June 18, 1928.

301 *Initial Trip by Air-Rail Made Today,* Iola Daily Register, Iola, Kansas, July 8, 1929.
302 *New Passenger Service Starts,* The Ada Evening News, Ada, Oklahoma, July 8, 1929.
303 Ibid.
304 Initial Trip by Air-Rail Made Today, *op. cit.*
305 *T.A.T. Ships to Have Radio Safety Factor,* Columbus Sunday Dispatch, December 23, 1928.
306 Ibid.
307 *Public Dedication Festivities Open,* Columbus Evening Dispatch, July 6, 1929. See also "Flying the Lindbergh Line: Then and Now, Robert F. Kirk, 2012.
308 *Expect 40,000 Visitors at New Airport During Day; 20,000 on Field Saturday,* Columbus Sunday Dispatch, July 7, 1929.
309 Ibid.
310 Public Dedication Festivities Open, *op. cit.*
311 *Transportation Epoch Marked in First Flights of T.A.T.,* The Clovis Journal, Clovis, NM, July 8, 1929; Robert J. Serling & George H. Foster, *Steel Rails and Silver Wings,* Hicksville: Weekend Chief Publishing Company, 2006, p. 86.
312 *The First Thirty Days,* TAT Plane Talk, August, 1929, Vol.1, No. 8.; and Robert J. Serling & George H. Foster, *Steel Rails and Silver Wings,* Hicksville: Weekend Chief Publishing Company, 2006, p. 86 -89.
313 *19 Women Fliers Span First Jump in Long Air Race,* The Morning Republican, Findlay, Ohio, August 19, 1929.
314 Ibid.
315 *1929 Air Race, Gene Nora Jessen,* International Women Pilots/99s News Magazine, 1999.
316 Ibid.
317 *Woman Pilot in Air Race Meets Death,* The Evening Tribune, Marysville, Ohio, August 29, 1929.
318 *Women Fliers in Air Derby, Forced Down by Mishaps,* Columbus Dispatch, August 21, 1929.
319 *Sabotage Charged Without Grounds,* Columbus Dispatch, August 22, 1929.

320 1929 Air Race, *op. cit.*
321 *Urges Women's Aviation Derby be Called Off,* Defiance Crescent News, Defiance, Ohio, August 23, 1929.
322 *Pittsburgh Flyer is Leading Women in Derby Event,* The Zanesville Signal, Zanesville, Ohio, August 24, 1929.
323 *Fifteen Women Expected Here,* Columbus Evening Dispatch, August 24, 1929.
324 *Earhart, Elder, Rasche Trail Mrs. Thaden to Port Columbus,* Columbus Sunday Dispatch, August 25, 1929.
325 *Ruth Nichols, Third in Race, Loses Place When Plane is Wrecked in Crash After Test Flight; Collides With Tractor,* Columbus Dispatch, August 26, 1929.
326 Ibid.
327 *Ladybirds Fly Away On Last Leg of Race,* Columbus Dispatch, August 26, 1929.
328 *Ladybirds Ending Derby Flight,* The Evening Gazette, Xenia, Ohio, August 26, 1929.
329 *High, Wide and Frightened,* Louise Thaden, Pathfinder Books, 1938. p. 43-62; 109-122.
330 *Log Book,* Foster A. Lane, Prop Press Associates, 1977. p. 45.
331 Ibid.
332 *Alex A. Boudreaux, Tuskegee Airman, Dies at 90,* Columbus Dispatch, February 24, 2011.
333 *Men in Business,* Columbus Dispatch, August, 1950.
334 *Jack Bolton, Columbus Airport Manager, Dies,* Newark Advocate, Newark, Ohio, October 21, 1968.
335 *Women in Aviation and Space History, Jerrie Geraldine Mock,* National Air and Space Archives, Smithsonian Institution.
336 *Jerri Mock, 88 First Woman to Circle Globe Solo, Dies,* The New York Times, October 5, 2014.
337 Ibid.
338 Jerri Mock, 88, *op. cit.*
339 *E. A. "Ed" Gillespie, The World's Oldest Active Test Pilot,* Journal, American Aviation Historical Society, Summer, 2001.
340 Ibid.

341 *Electronic Communication*, Scott Gillespie, Executor of Ed Gillespie Estate, 2019.

342 *Profile of John Glenn* NASA, <http://www.nasa.gov/content/profile-of-john-glenn>

343 *The John Glenn, Jr. Oral History Project, Oral History Interview 1 with Senator John Glenn, Jr,.* October 25, 1996, p 41-42, & 59, Brian R. Williams (Interviewer).

344 *The Wartime Journals of Charles A. Lindbergh,* Charles Lindbergh, Harcourt Brace Jovanovich, Inc. New York, p 816, 1970.

345 From a conversation and personal notes and photo collection of Nolan Leatherman, longtime employee of North American Aviation, Columbus Ohio, 2018.

346 Ibid.

347 Ibid.

348 Photo from the Collection of Captain Don Peters. Columbus, Ohio 2018. Photo used by permission from Captain Don Peters.

SELECTED BIBLIOGRAPHY

Ada Evening News, Ada, Oklahoma, July 8, 1929.

Chronicle – Telegram, Elyra, Ohio. November 9, 1927.

Clovis Journal, Clovis, New Mexico, July 8, 1929.

Columbus Dispatch, Columbus, Ohio.

Defiance Crescent News, Defiance, Ohio, August 23, 1929.

Evening Gazette, Xenia, Ohio, August 26, 1929.

Evening Independence, Massillon, Ohio, October 30, 1928.

Evening Tribune, Marysville, Ohio, October 25, 1928.

Herald-Star, Steubenville, Ohio, November 27, 1928.

Iola Daily Register, Iola, Kansas, July 8, 1929.

Journal American Aviation Historical Society, *E. A. "Ed" Gillespie, The World's Oldest Active Test Pilot,* Summer, 2001.

Kessner, Thomas, *The Flight of the Century*, Oxford University Press, 2010.

Kirk, Robert, *Flying the Lindbergh Line: Then and Now,* AuthorHouse, 2013.

Larkins, William T., *The Ford Tri-Motor 1926 – 1992*, Schiffer.

Lane, Foster A., *Log Book*, Prop Press Associates, 1977.

Las Vegas Daily Optic, Las Vegas, New Mexico, February 18, 1929.

Lindbergh Charles A., *"WE"*, Grosset & Dunlap, NY, 1927.

Lindbergh, Charles A., *The Wartime Journals of Charles Lindbergh*, Harcourt, Brace, Jovanovich, Inc., New York, 1970.

Lindbergh, Charles A., *The Spirit of St. Louis*, Charles Scribner's Sons, New York, 1953.

Stork, Ernest H., *Columbus Builds an Airport: Port Columbus "America's Greatest Air Harbor*, Unpublished work, Columbus Metropolitan Library, Columbus, Ohio.

Sandusky Register, Sandusky, Ohio, December 9, 1928.

Serling, Robert J. and George H. Foster, *Steel Rails and Sliver Wings*, Hicksville: Weekend Chief Publishing Company, 2006.

Thaden, Louise, *High Wide and Frightened*, Pathfinder Books, 1938.

Morning Republican, Findlay, Ohio, August 19, 1929.

Newark Advocate, Newark, Ohio, October 21, 1968.

New York Times.

Waterloo Iowa Courier, Waterloo Iowa, July 10, 1929.

Zanesville Signal, Zanesville, Ohio, August 24, 1929.

Printed in the United States
By Bookmasters